God's Love for LGBTQI

God's Love for LGBTQI
By Marie White

Categories: CHRISTIAN BOOKS & BIBLES > CHRISTIAN LIVING > SOCIAL ISSUES

Copyright © 2015 Marie White

ISBN-13: 978-1522944027
ISBN-10: 1522944028
All rights reserved.

Scripture taken from the New Century Version®. Copyright © 2005 by Thomas Nelson. Used by permission. All rights reserved.

Scripture quotations marked HCSB are taken from the Holman Christian Standard Bible®, Copyright © 1999, 2000, 2002, 2003, 2009 by Holman Bible Publishers. Used by permission. Holman Christian Standard Bible®, Holman CSB®, and HCSB® are federally registered trademarks of Holman Bible Publishers.

THE HOLY BIBLE, NEW INTERNATIONAL VERSION®, NIV® Copyright © 1973, 1978, 1984, 2011 by Biblica, Inc.® Used by permission. All rights reserved worldwide.

Scripture taken from the NEW AMERICAN STANDARD BIBLE®, Copyright © 1960,1962,1963,1968,1971,1972,1973,1975,1977,1995 by The Lockman Foundation. Used by permission.

Scripture taken from the New King James Version®. Copyright © 1982 by Thomas Nelson. Used by permission. All rights reserved.

Scriptures taken from the Holy Bible, New International Reader's Version®, NIrV® Copyright © 1995, 1996, 1998 by Biblica, Inc.™ Used by permission of Zondervan. www.zondervan.com The "NIrV" and "New International Reader's Version" are trademarks registered in the United States Patent and Trademark Office by Biblica, Inc.™

Scripture quotations marked (ESV) are from The Holy Bible, English Standard Version® (ESV®), copyright © 2001 by Crossway, a publishing ministry of Good News Publishers. Used by permission. All rights reserved.

Scripture taken from the International Children's Bible®. Copyright © 1986, 1988, 1999 by Thomas Nelson. Used by permission. All rights reserved.

Scripture taken from the Modern English Version. Copyright © 2014 by Military Bible Association. Used by permission. All rights reserved.

Scripture quotations marked (NLT) are taken from the Holy Bible, New Living Translation, copyright © 1996, 2004, 2007 by Tyndale House Foundation. Used by permission of Tyndale House Publishers, Inc., Carol Stream, Illinois 60188. All rights reserved.

Scripture quotations marked (CEV) are from the Contemporary English Version Copyright © 1991, 1992, 1995 by American Bible Society, Used by Permission.

Scripture quotations marked (ERV) are taken from the HOLY BIBLE: EASY-TO-READ VERSION © 2014 by Bible League International. and used by permission.

Scripture quotations marked (GNT) are from the Good News Translation in Today's English Version- Second Edition Copyright © 1992 by American Bible Society. Used by Permission.

Quotations marked GW, Scripture is taken from GOD'S WORD®, © 1995 God's Word to the Nations. Used by permission of Baker Publishing Group.

Scripture quotations marked (TLB) are taken from The Living Bible copyright © 1971. Used by permission of Tyndale House Publishers, Inc., Carol Stream, Illinois 60188. All rights reserved.

Scripture quotations taken from the Amplified® Bible, Copyright © 2015 by The Lockman Foundation. Used by permission. (www.Lockman.org)

Scripture taken from the Holy Bible: International Standard Version®. Copyright © 1996-forever by The ISV Foundation. ALL RIGHTS RESERVED INTERNATIONALLY. Used by permission.

Scripture quotations marked NRSV are from the New Revised Standard Version Bible, copyright © 1989 the Division of Christian Education of the National Council of the Churches of Christ in the United States of America. Used by permission. All rights reserved.

GRAPHICS BY AJAY SHRIVASTAVA & VECTEEZY.COM

FOR YOU

_____ you are loved with an everlasting love. Never forget that God made you. He knit you together in your mother's womb (Psalm 139:13∞) and has great plans for you (Jeremiah 29:11∞.)

Live your life to the fullest. Become who you were meant to be and remember that you are loved.

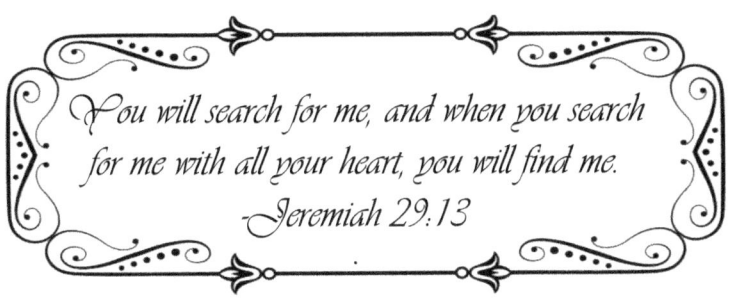

You will search for me, and when you search for me with all your heart, you will find me.
—Jeremiah 29:13

CONTENTS

Safety	1
Freedom	13
Rest	23
Help	31
Peace	45
Equality	53
Trust	63
Sorrow	73
Love	85
Forgiveness	97
Joy	105
Hope	115
Eternity	129
Jesus Said	135
God	151
Common Questions	163

A Glimpse Into The Bible	169
Joseph	171
The Ten Commandments	186
Ruth	189
Job	192
Psalms	197
Ecclesiastes	203
Paul	206
Ending Prayer	213
Recommended Reading	217

Dedicated to the people whom God has graciously given me, my family and friends. It has been encouraging to watch you support each other with genuine love. You have shown me that we grow stronger by bearing each other's burdens.

Most of all I dedicate this to the love of my life. You are my strong warrior and biggest supporter. I thank God for you, each day.

Safety

God is not an employer looking for employees. He is an eagle looking for people who will take refuge under his wings. He is looking for people who will leave father and mother and homeland or anything else that may hold them back from a life of love under the wings of Jesus. -John Piper

I prayed to the Lord, and he answered me. He freed me from all my fears. Psalm 34:4 GNT

Do not be afraid—I am with you! I am your God—let nothing terrify you! I will make you strong and help you; I will protect you and save you.
Isaiah 41:10∞ GNT

The Lord is a place of safety for those who have been treated badly. He keeps them safe in times of trouble. Lord, those who know you will trust in you. You have never deserted those who look to you. Psalm 9:9-10∞ NIRV

Be merciful to me, O God, be merciful, because I come to you for safety. In the shadow of your wings I find protection until the raging storms are over.
Psalm 57:1∞ GNT

∞ Old Testament   Ω New Testament

Deliver me from mine enemies, O my God: defend me from them that rise up against me. Psalm 59:1∞ KJV

Fearing people is a dangerous trap, but trusting the Lord means safety. Proverbs 29:25∞ NLT

Listen closely to me; rescue me quickly. Be a rock of refuge for me, a mountain fortress to save me. Psalm 31:2∞ HCSB

Every word of God proves true. He is a shield to all who come to him for protection. Proverbs 30:5∞ NLT

I keep my eyes always on the Lord. With him at my right hand, I will not be shaken. Psalm 16:8∞ NIV

He will cover you with his feathers. He will shelter you with his wings. His faithful promises are your armor and protection. Do not be afraid of the terrors of the night, nor the arrow that flies in the day. Do not dread the disease that stalks in darkness, nor the disaster that strikes at midday. Psalm 91:4-6∞ NLT

"Lord, help!" they cried in their trouble, and he saved them from their distress. He led them from the darkness and deepest gloom; he snapped their chains. Let them praise the Lord for his great love and for the wonderful things he has done for them. Psalm 107:13-16∞ NLT

But those who listen to me will live in safety. They will be at ease and have no fear of being harmed. Proverbs 1:33∞ NIRV

This poor man cried, and the Lord heard him, and saved him out of all his troubles. Psalm 34:6∞ KJV

These two things cannot change: God cannot lie when he says something, and he cannot lie when he makes an oath. So these two things are a great help to us who have come to God for safety. They encourage us to hold on to the hope that is ours.
Hebrews 6:18 Ω ERV

Find out for yourself how good the Lord is. Happy are those who find safety with him. Psalm 34:8∞ GNT

Of Benjamin he said: The beloved of the Lord will dwell in safety by Him, and the Lord will protect him all day long; he will dwell between His shoulders. Deuteronomy 33:12∞ MEV

Are not five sparrows sold for two farthings, and not one of them is forgotten before God? But even the very hairs of your head are all numbered. Fear not therefore: ye are of more value than many sparrows. Luke 12:6-7 Ω KJV

You, Lord, are all I want! You are my choice, and you keep me safe. Psalm 16:5∞ CEV

And the Lord shall help them, and deliver them: he shall deliver them from the wicked, and save them, because they trust in him. Psalm 37:40∞ KJV

The Lord your God is supreme over all gods and over all powers. He is great and mighty, and he is to be obeyed. He does not show partiality, and he does not accept bribes. Deuteronomy 10:17∞ GNT

So my heart and soul will be very happy. Even my body will live in safety, Psalm 16:9∞ ERV

Redeem me from man's oppression, that I may keep your precepts. Psalm 119:134∞ ESV

You give peace of mind to all who love your Law. Nothing can make them fall. Psalm 119:165∞ CEV

If it is not the Lord who builds a house, the builders are wasting their time. If it is not the Lord who watches over the city, the guards are wasting their time.
Psalm 127:1∞ ERV

I trust in the Lord for safety. How foolish of you to say to me, "Fly away like a bird to the mountains, because the wicked have drawn their bows and aimed their arrows to shoot from the shadows at good people.
Psalm 11:1-2∞ GNT

Protect me, O God; I trust in you for safety. Psalm 16:1° GNT

He is my steadfast love and my fortress, my stronghold and my deliverer, my shield and he in whom I take refuge, who subdues peoples under me. Psalm 144:2∞ ESV

The Lord reached down from above and took me; he pulled me from the deep water. He saved me from my powerful enemies, from those who hated me, because they were too strong for me. They attacked me at my time of trouble, but the Lord supported me. He took me to a safe place. Because he delights in me, he saved me. Psalm 18:16-19∞ NCV

You hide them in the safety of your presence from the plots of others; in a safe shelter you hide them from the insults of their enemies.

Psalm 31:20∞ GNT

Do not be a terror to me; you are my place of safety when trouble comes. Jeremiah 17:17∞ GNT

Reveal your wonderful love and save me; at your side I am safe from my enemies. Psalm 17:7∞ GNT

But he saves the needy from the sword of their mouth and from the hand of the mighty.
Job 5:15∞ ESV

Their hearts are secure. They aren't afraid. In the end they will see their enemies destroyed
Psalm 112:8∞ NIRV

When I was secure, I said, "I will never be shaken."
Psalm 30:6∞ HCSB

The Lord is my rock, my protection, my Savior. My God is my rock. I can run to him for safety. He is my shield and my saving strength, my defender. I will call to the Lord, who is worthy of praise, and I will be saved from my enemies.
Psalm 18:2-3∞ NCV

Make sure you are going the right way, and nothing will make you fall. Proverbs 4:26∞ ERV

I will call on the Lord, who is worthy to be praised: so shall I be saved from mine enemies. 2 Samuel 22:4° KJV

I know that the Lord secures justice for the poor and upholds the cause of the needy. Psalm 140:12∞ NIV

Those who fear the Lord are secure; he will be a refuge for their children. Proverbs 14:26∞ NLT

The Lord is near the brokenhearted; He saves those crushed in spirit. Psalm 34:18∞ HCSB

The Lord says, "I will make my people strong with power from me! They will go wherever they wish, and wherever they go they will be under my personal care." Zechariah 10:12∞ TLB

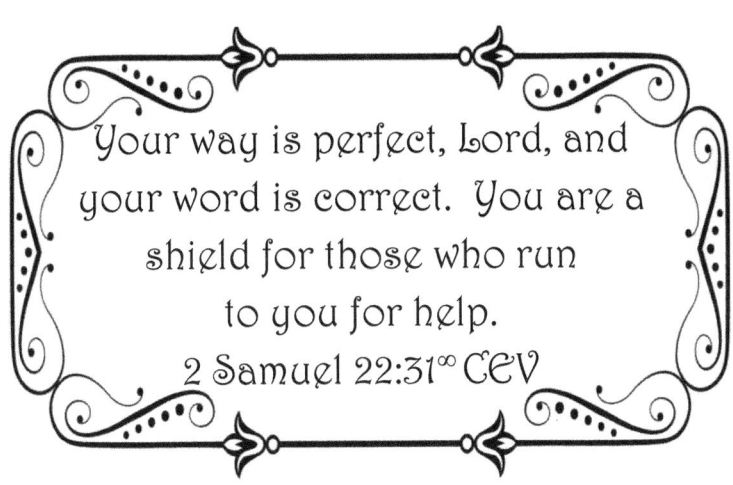

Your way is perfect, Lord, and your word is correct. You are a shield for those who run to you for help.
2 Samuel 22:31 CEV

In peace I will lie down and sleep,
for you alone, Lord,
make me dwell in safety.
Psalm 4:8 NIV

God has not forgotten you.

You will find safety under his wings.

GOD'S LOVE FOR LGBTQI

Freedom

No amount of determination will bring freedom. We're going to learn to be victorious by surrendering our lives completely to the Spirit of God, not by gritting our teeth and trying harder. -Beth Moore

GOD'S LOVE FOR LGBTQI

Through him and through faith in him we can approach God. We can come to him freely. We can come without fear.
Ephesians 3:12 Ω NIRV

God is gently calling you from the jaws of trouble to an open place of freedom where he has set your table full of the best food. Job 36:16 ∞ NCV

Let us praise the Lord, the God of Israel, because he has come to help his people and has given them freedom. Luke 1:68 Ω NCV

He is so rich in kindness and grace that he purchased our freedom with the blood of his Son and forgave our sins. He has showered his kindness on us, along with all wisdom and understanding.

Ephesians 1:7-8 Ω NLT

I will sweep your sins away as if they were a cloud. I will blow them away as if they were the morning mist. Return to me. Then I will set you free."
Isaiah 44:22 ∞ NIRV

To the Jews who had believed him, Jesus said, "If you hold to my teaching, you are really my disciples. Then you will know the truth, and the truth will set you free." John 8:31-32 Ω NIV

So if the Son sets you free, you will be free indeed.
John 8:36 Ω *ESV*

And I will walk at liberty, For I seek and deeply long for Your precepts. Psalm 119:45 ∞ AMP

You are my strong fortress, and you set me free.
2 Samuel 22:33 ∞ CEV

And he has taken our sins as far away from us as the east is from the west.
Psalm 103:12 ∞ ERV

But when anyone turns to the Lord, the veil is taken away. Now the Lord is the Holy Spirit. And where the Spirit of the Lord is, freedom is also there.
2 Corinthians 3:16-17 ῼ NIRV

But I wipe away your sins because of who I am. And so, I will forget the wrongs you have done.
Isaiah 43:25 ∞ CEV

Anyone who belongs to Christ is a new person. The past is forgotten, and everything is new.
2 Corinthians 5:17 ῼ CEV

We have freedom now, because Christ made us free. So stand strong. Do not change and go back into the slavery of the law. Galatians 5:1 ῼ NCV

If you are a follower of Christ Jesus, it makes no difference whether you are circumcised or not. All that matters is your faith that makes you love others. Galatians 5:6 ῼ CEV

My friends, you were chosen to be free. So don't use your freedom as an excuse to do anything you want. Use it as an opportunity to serve each other with love. All that the Law says can be summed up in the command to love others as much as you love yourself.
Galatians 5:13-14 CEV

Doing right brings freedom to honest people, but those who are not trustworthy will be caught by their own desires.

Proverbs 11:6 NCV

But the one who looks at the perfect law of freedom and remains committed to it—thereby demonstrating that he is not a forgetful hearer but a doer of what that law requires—will be blessed in what he does.
James 1:25 ISV

And the scroll of the prophet Isaiah was handed to him. Unrolling it, he found the place where it is written: "The Spirit of the Lord is on me, because he has anointed me to proclaim good news to the poor. He has sent me to proclaim freedom for the prisoners and recovery of sight for the blind, to set the oppressed free, to proclaim the year of the Lord's favor." Luke 4:17-19 Ω NIV

If you confess with your mouth, "Jesus is Lord," and believe in your heart that God raised Him from the dead, you will be saved. One believes with the heart, resulting in righteousness, and one confesses with the mouth, resulting in salvation. Now the Scripture says, Everyone who believes on Him will not be put to shame, for there is no distinction between Jew and Greek, since the same Lord of all is rich to all who call on Him. For everyone who calls on the name of the Lord will be saved. But how can they call on Him they have not believed in? And how can they believe without hearing about Him? And how can they hear without a preacher? And how can they preach unless they are sent? As it is written: How beautiful are the feet of those who announce the gospel of good things!
Romans 10:9-15 Ω HCSB

GOD'S LOVE FOR LGBTQI

Christ died for us at a time when we were helpless and sinful. No one is really willing to die for an honest person, though someone might be willing to die for a truly good person. But God showed how much he loved us by having Christ die for us, even though we were sinful. But there is more! Now that God has accepted us because Christ sacrificed his life's blood, we will also be kept safe from God's anger. Even when we were God's enemies, he made peace with us, because his Son died for us. Yet something even greater than friendship is ours. Now that we are at peace with God, we will be saved by his Son's life.

Romans 5:6-10 Ω CEV

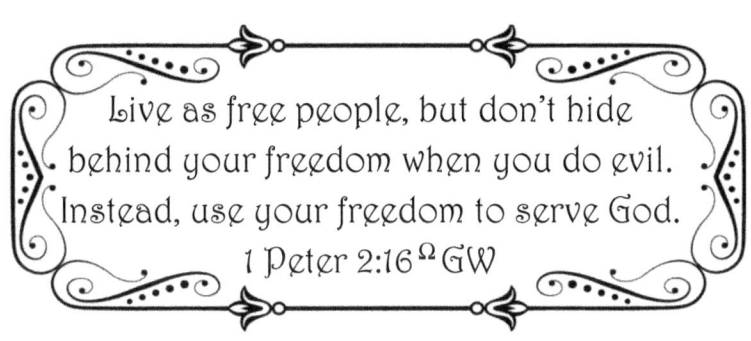

Live as free people, but don't hide behind your freedom when you do evil. Instead, use your freedom to serve God. 1 Peter 2:16 Ω GW

So now anyone who is in Christ Jesus is not judged guilty. Romans 8:1 Ω ERV

You are promised freedom.

God's love will set you free.

… GOD'S LOVE FOR LGBTQI

Rest

If you look at the world, you'll be distressed. If you look within, you'll be depressed. If you look at God you'll be at rest. –Corrie ten Boom

GOD'S LOVE FOR LGBTQI

"Blessed are those who mourn, for they shall be comforted. Matthew 5:4 Ω NASB

Cast all your anxiety on him because he cares for you.
1 Peter 5:7 Ω *NIV*

No temptation has overtaken you except such as is common to man; but God is faithful, who will not allow you to be tempted beyond what you are able, but with the temptation will also make the way of escape, that you may be able to bear it.
1 Corinthians 10:13 Ω NKJV

Then He replied, "My presence will go with you, and I will give you rest."
Exodus 33:14 ∞ HCSB

Trust in the Lord with all your heart. Do not depend on your own understanding. In all your ways obey him. Then he will make your paths smooth and straight.
Proverbs 3:5-6∞ NIRV

He heals the brokenhearted and binds up their wounds. Psalm 147:3∞ NASB

"Come to me, all of you who are tired from carrying heavy loads, and I will give you rest. Matthew 11:28 Ω GNT

Take my yoke and put it on you, and learn from me, because I am gentle and humble in spirit; and you will find rest. Matthew 11:29 Ω GNT

Don't worry about anything; instead, pray about everything. Tell God what you need, and thank him for all he has done. Philippians 4:6 Ω NLT

Whoever rests in the shadow of the Most High God will be kept safe by the Mighty One. Psalm 91:1 NIRV

"Forget the former things; do not dwell on the past. Isaiah 43:18 NIV

Be strong and courageous; don't be terrified or afraid of them. For it is the Lord your God who goes with you; He will not leave you or forsake you." Deuteronomy 31:6 HCSB

Send your light and your truth. Let them guide me. Let them bring me to your holy mountain and to your dwelling place. Psalm 43:3 GW

The entrance of thy words giveth light; it giveth understanding unto the simple. Psalm 119:130 KJV

GOD'S LOVE FOR LGBTQI

The Lord is my shepherd; I have everything I need. He lets me rest in fields of green grass and leads me to quiet pools of fresh water. He gives me new strength. He guides me in the right paths, as he has promised. Even if I go through the deepest darkness, I will not be afraid, Lord, for you are with me. Your shepherd's rod and staff protect me. You prepare a banquet for me, where all my enemies can see me; you welcome me as an honored guest and fill my cup to the brim. I know that your goodness and love will be with me all my life; and your house will be my home as long as I live.

Psalm 23:1-6 GNT

The Lord my God has now given me rest all around; there is no enemy or crisis.
1 Kings 5:4 HCSB

Praise the Lord! He has kept his promise and given us peace. Every good thing he promised to his servant Moses has happened. 1 Kings 8:56 CEV

To God you are priceless.

You can rest with Him.

GOD'S LOVE FOR LGBTQI

Help

I read a story about an old gentlemen who was known for his godly life. Someone asked him one day, "What do you do when you are tempted, old man?" He replied, "I just look up to Heaven and say, 'Lord, your property is in danger.'" -Greg Laurie

GOD'S LOVE FOR LGBTQI

In my distress I cried unto the Lord, and he heard me. Psalm 120:1 KJV

From the depths of my despair I call to you, Lord. Hear my cry, O Lord; listen to my call for help! Psalm 130:1-2∞ GNT

Lord, be pleased to deliver me; hurry to help me, Lord.
Psalm 40:13∞ HCSB

I have a lot of enemies, Lord. Many fight against me and say, "God won't rescue you!" But you are my shield, and you give me victory and great honor.
I pray to you, and you answer from your sacred hill. Psalm 3:1-4∞ CEV

My help will come from the Lord, who made heaven and earth.
Psalm 121:2∞ GNT

GOD'S LOVE FOR LGBTQI

You are my God and protector. Please answer my prayer. I was in terrible distress, but you set me free. Now have pity and listen as I pray. Psalm 4:1∞ CEV

You are my hiding place and my shield,
I hope in Your word.
Psalm 119:114° MEV

Go away, all you who do evil, for the Lord has heard my weeping. The Lord has heard my plea; the Lord will answer my prayer. Psalm 6:8-9∞ NLT

I prayed to the Lord, and he answered me. He freed me from all my fears. Psalm 34:4∞ NLT

With all my heart I call to you; answer me, Lord, and I will obey your commands! I call to you; save me, and I will keep your laws. Psalm 119:145-146∞ GNT

When you beg the Lord for help, he will answer, "Here I am!" Don't mistreat others or falsely accuse them or say something cruel. Give your food to the hungry and care for the homeless. Then your light will shine in the dark; your darkest hour will be like the noonday sun. Isaiah 58:9-10∞ CEV

Have mercy on us, Lord, have mercy on us, for we have endured no end of contempt. We have endured no end of ridicule from the arrogant, of contempt from the proud. Psalm 123:3-4∞ NIV

God is our refuge and strength, a very present help in trouble. Psalm 46:1∞ KJV

Two are better than one; because they have a good reward for their labour. For if they fall, the one will lift up his fellow: but woe to him that is alone when he falleth; for he hath not another to help him up. Ecclesiastes 4:9-10 Ω KJV

O Lord my God, in You I put my trust; save me from all those who persecute me, and deliver me, lest they tear my soul like a lion, rending it in pieces, while there is none to deliver. Psalm 7:1-2∞ MEV

GOD'S LOVE FOR LGBTQI

Let us give thanks to the God and Father of our Lord Jesus Christ, the merciful Father, the God from whom all help comes! He helps us in all our troubles, so that we are able to help others who have all kinds of troubles, using the same help that we ourselves have received from God. Just as we have a share in Christ's many sufferings, so also through Christ we share in God's great help.
2 Corinthians 1:3-5 ♎ GNT

So he is able always to save those who come to God through him because he always lives, asking God to help them. Hebrews 7:25 ♎ NCV

Listen to my words, O Lord, and hear my sighs. Listen to my cry for help, my God and king! I pray to you, O Lord; Psalm 5:1-2∞ GNT

I long for you to rescue me! Your word is my only hope. Psalm 119:81∞ CEV

Arise, O Lord, in your anger; lift yourself up against the fury of my enemies; awake for me; you have appointed a judgment. Psalm 7:6∞ ESV

Commit your works to the Lord And your plans will be established. Proverbs 16:3∞ NASB

O Lord, listen to my prayer. Open your ears to hear my urgent requests. Answer me because you are faithful and righteous. Do not take me to court for judgment, because there is no one alive who is righteous in your presence. Psalm 143:1-2 GW

Lord, I call upon You; hurry to me. Listen to my voice when I call to You. Psalm 141:1 AMP

Nevertheless, my Lord God, please pay attention to my prayer for mercy. Listen to my cry for help as I pray to you. 2 Chronicles 6:19 GW

Give praise to the Lord; he has heard my cry for help. Psalm 28:6 GNT

Be gracious to me, O Lord. See what I suffer from those who hate me; you are the one who lifts me up from the gates of death. Psalm 9:13 NRSV

Lord, rise up and punish the wicked. Don't forget those who need help. Why do wicked people hate God? They say to themselves, "God won't punish us." Lord, surely you see these cruel and evil things; look at them and do something. People in trouble look to you for help. You are the one who helps the orphans. Break the power of wicked people. Punish them for the evil they have done. The Lord is King forever and ever. Destroy from your land those nations that do not worship you. Lord, you have heard what the poor people want. Do what they ask, and listen to them. Protect the orphans and put an end to suffering so they will no longer be afraid of evil people.

Psalm 10:12-18 NCV

Behold, the Lord's hand is not so short That it cannot save, Nor His ear so impaired That it cannot hear. Isaiah 59:1∞ AMP

Please listen to my prayer and my cry for help, as I lift my hands toward your holy temple. Psalm 28:2∞ CEV

I had said in my alarm, "I am cut off from your sight." But you heard the voice of my pleas for mercy when I cried to you for help.
Psalm 31:22∞ ESV

Let us therefore come boldly unto the throne of grace, that we may obtain mercy, and find grace to help in time of need. Hebrews 4:16 Ω KJV

Rejoice not against me, O mine enemy: when I fall, I shall arise; when I sit in darkness, the Lord shall be a light unto me. Micah 7:8∞ KJV

Lord, you are loyal to those who are loyal, and you are good to those who are good. You are pure to those who are pure, but you are against those who are bad. You save the humble, but you bring down those who are proud. Lord, you give light to my lamp. My God brightens the darkness around me. With your help I can attack an army. With God's help I can jump over a wall. The ways of God are without fault. The Lord's words are pure. He is a shield to those who trust him. Who is God? Only the Lord. Who is the Rock? Only our God. God is my protection. He makes my way free from fault. He makes me like a deer that does not stumble; he helps me stand on the steep mountains. He trains my hands for battle so my arms can bend a bronze bow. You protect me with your saving shield. You support me with your right hand. You have stooped to make me great. You give me a better way to live, so I live as you want me to.
Psalm 18:25-36 NCV

The ropes of death came around me; the deadly rivers overwhelmed me. The ropes of death wrapped around me. The traps of death were before me. In my trouble I called to the Lord. I cried out to my God for help. From his temple he heard my voice; my call for help reached his ears. Psalm 18:4-6∞ NCV

The Lord lives!
May my Rock be praised.
Praise the God who saves me!
God gives me victory over my enemies
and brings people under my rule.
He saves me from my enemies.
You set me over those who hate me.
You saved me from violent people.
So I will praise you, Lord, among the nations.
I will sing praises to your name.
Psalm 18:46-49∞ NCV

Save me, Lord, because the good people are all gone; no true believers are left on earth. Everyone lies to his neighbors; they say one thing and mean another. The Lord will stop those flattering lips and cut off those bragging tongues. They say, "Our tongues will help us win. We can say what we wish; no one is our master." But the Lord says, "I will now rise up, because the poor are being hurt. Because of the moans of the helpless, I will give them the help they want." The Lord's words are pure, like silver purified by fire, like silver purified seven times over. Lord, you will keep us safe; you will always protect us from such people. Psalm 12:1-7 NCV

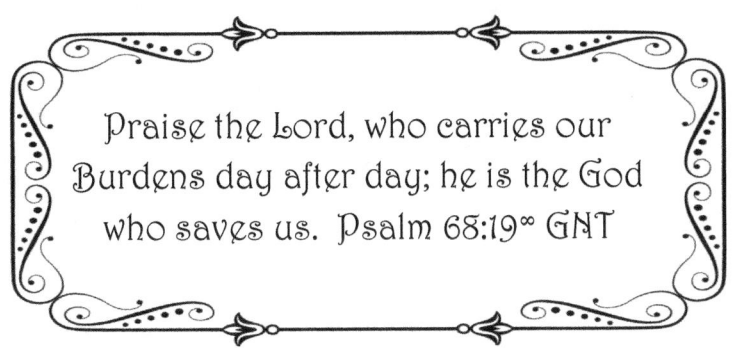

Praise the Lord, who carries our Burdens day after day; he is the God who saves us. Psalm 68:19∞ GNT

Therefore don't worry about tomorrow, because tomorrow will worry about itself. Each day has enough trouble of its own.
Matthew 6:34 Ω HCSB

You are not alone.

God will answer you.

GOD'S LOVE FOR LGBTQI

Peace

And in despair I bowed my head;
"There is no peace on earth," I said;
"For hate is strong,
And mocks the song
Of peace on earth, good-will to men!"
Then pealed the bells more loud and deep:
"God is not dead, nor doth he sleep!
The Wrong shall fail,
the Right prevail,
With peace on earth, good-will to men!"
-Henry Wadsworth Longfellow

I leave you peace. It is my own peace I give you. I give you peace in a different way than the world does. So don't be troubled. Don't be afraid.
John 14:27 ERV

God, you give true peace to people who depend on you, to those who trust in you.
Isaiah 26:3 ERV

We have been made right with God because of our faith. So we have peace with God through our Lord Jesus Christ. Romans 5:1 ERV

But he told me: "My kindness is all you need. My power is strongest when you are weak." So I will brag even more about my weaknesses in order that Christ's power will live in me. Therefore, I accept weakness, mistreatment, hardship, persecution, and difficulties suffered for Christ. It's clear that when I'm weak, I'm strong. 2 Corinthians 12:9-10 GW

I will listen to you, Lord God, because you promise peace to those who are faithful and no longer foolish.
Psalm 85:8∞ CEV

Those who love your teachings will find true peace. Nothing can make them fall. Psalm 119:165∞ ERV

There is nothing better for a man than to eat and drink and tell himself that his labor is good. This also I have seen that it is from the hand of God. For who can eat and who can have enjoyment without Him?
Ecclesiastes 2:24-25∞ NASB

I love your word. Time and again it has been proven true. Psalm 119:140∞ ERV

Obey God and be at peace with him; this is the way to happiness. Job 21:22∞ NCV

Depart from evil, and do good; seek peace, and pursue it. Psalm 34:14∞ KJV

Peace of mind makes the body healthy, but jealousy is like a cancer. Proverbs 14:30∞ ERV

When a man's ways please the Lord, he maketh even his enemies to be at peace with him. Proverbs 16:7∞ KJV

I pray that the God who gives hope will fill you with much joy and peace as you trust in him. Then you will have more and more hope, and it will flow out of you by the power of the Holy Spirit. Romans 15:13 $^\Omega$

Late into the night I stay awake to think about your word. Psalm 119:148∞ ERV

Keep your life free from love of money, and be content with what you have, for he has said, "I will never leave you nor forsake you." Hebrews 13:5 $^\Omega$ ESV

Lord, You will establish peace for us, for You have also done all our work for us. Isaiah 26:12∞HCSB

"May the Lord bless you and keep you. May the Lord show you his kindness and have mercy on you. May the Lord watch over you and give you peace."
Numbers 6:24-26∞ NCV

If only you had paid attention to My commands.
Then your peace would have been like a river,
and your righteousness like the waves of the sea.
Isaiah 48:18 ∞ HCSB

If possible, on your part, live at peace
with everyone. Romans 12:18 Ω HCSB

For the kingdom of God is not meat and drink; but
righteousness, and peace, and joy in the Holy Ghost.
Romans 14:17 Ω KJV

For God is not the author of confusion, but of
peace, as in all churches of the saints.
1 Corinthians 14:33 Ω KJV

And He came and preached peace to you who were
far away, and peace to those who were near;
Ephesians 2:17 Ω NASB

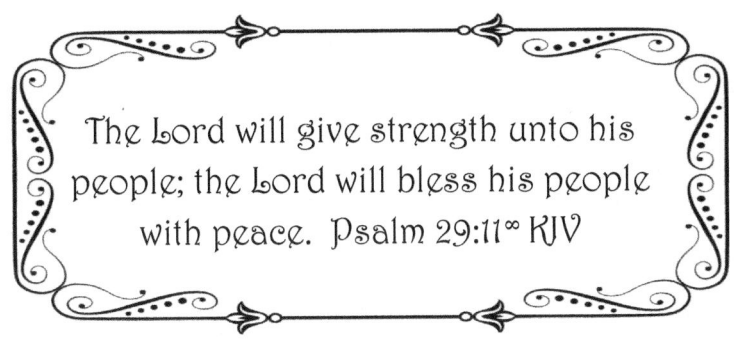

The Lord will give strength unto his people; the Lord will bless his people with peace. Psalm 29:11∞ KJV

For a child has been born for us, a son given to us; authority rests upon his shoulders; and he is named Wonderful Counselor, Mighty God, Everlasting Father, Prince of Peace. Isaiah 9:6∞ NRSV

You were not made to worry.

There is peace with God.

GOD'S LOVE FOR LGBTQI

Equality

Thunderously, inarguably, the Sermon on the Mount proves that before God we all stand on level ground: murderers and temper-throwers, adulterers and lusters, thieves and coveters. We are all desperate, and that is in fact the only state appropriate to a human being who wants to know God. Having fallen from the absolute Ideal, we have nowhere to land but in the safety net of absolute grace. –Philip Yancey

GOD'S LOVE FOR LGBTQI

Now, in Christ, it doesn't matter if you are a Jew or a Greek, a slave or free, male or female. You are all the same in Christ Jesus.
Galatians 3:28 Ω ERV

You pray to God and call him Father, and he judges each person's work equally. So while you are here on earth, you should live with respect for God.
1 Peter 1:17 Ω NCV

If any of you lacks wisdom, you should ask God, who gives generously to all without finding fault, and it will be given to you.
James 1:5 Ω NIV

No one in heaven is equal to the Lord. None of the "gods" can compare to the Lord.
Psalm 89:6 ∞ ERV

I am the good shepherd, and the good shepherd gives up his life for his sheep.
John 10:11 Ω CEV

"Who will you compare Me to, or who is My equal?" asks the Holy One. Isaiah 40:25 HCSB

A thief comes only to rob, kill, and destroy. I came so that everyone would have life, and have it in its fullest. John 10:10 CEV

My sheep know my voice, and I know them. They follow me, and I give them eternal life, so that they will never be lost. No one can snatch them out of my hand. John 10:27-28 CEV

for all have sinned and fall short of the glory of God. Romans 3:23 NASB

"What I'm about to tell you is true. Anyone who hears my word and believes him who sent me has eternal life. They will not be judged. They have crossed over from death to life. John 5:24 NIRV

But as many as received Him, to them He gave the right to become children of God, to those who believe in His name: John 1:12 NKJV

Masters, give unto your servants that which is just and equal; knowing that ye also have a Master in heaven. Colossians 4:1 KJV

In your lives you must think and act like Christ Jesus. Christ himself was like God in everything. But he did not think that being equal with God was something to be used for his own benefit. But he gave up his place with God and made himself nothing. He was born as a man and became like a servant.
Philippians 2:5-7$^\Omega$ NCV

When I look at the night sky and see the work of your fingers— the moon and the stars you set in place— what are mere mortals that you should think about them, human beings that you should care for them? Yet you made them only a little lower than God and crowned them with glory and honor. You gave them charge of everything you made, putting all things under their authority— the flocks and the herds and all the wild animals, the birds in the sky, the fish in the sea, and everything that swims the ocean currents. O Lord, our Lord, your majestic name fills the earth! Psalm 8:3-9$^\infty$ NLT

Jesus answered, "Healthy people don't need a doctor, but sick people do. I didn't come to invite good people to turn to God. I came to invite sinners."
Luke 5:31-32$^\Omega$ CEV

Christ died for us at a time when we were helpless and sinful. No one is really willing to die for an honest person, though someone might be willing to die for a truly good person. But God showed how much he loved us by having Christ die for us, even though we were sinful. But there is more! Now that God has accepted us because Christ sacrificed his life's blood, we will also be kept safe from God's anger. Even when we were God's enemies, he made peace with us, because his Son died for us. Yet something even greater than friendship is ours. Now that we are at peace with God, we will be saved by his Son's life.

Romans 5:6-10 $^\Omega$ CEV

But now Christ has brought you back to God by dying in his physical body. He did this so that you could come into God's presence without sin, fault, or blame.
Colossians 1:22 ῼ GW

You are confused.
You think the clay is equal to the potter.
You think that an object can tell the person who made it,
"You didn't make me."
This is like a pot telling its maker,
"You don't know anything."
Isaiah 29:16° ICB

We do not want you to have troubles while other people are at ease. We want everything to be equal.
2 Corinthians 8:13 ῼ ICB

Suppose I say to a sinful person, 'You can be sure you will die.' And then they turn away from their sin. They do what is fair and right. They return things they take to make sure loans are repaid. They give back what they have stolen. They obey my rules that give life. They do not do what is evil. Then you can be sure they will live. They will not die. None of the sins they have committed will be held against them. They have done what is fair and right. So you can be sure they will live. "In spite of that, your people say, 'What the Lord does isn't fair.' But it is what you do that is not fair. Suppose a godly person stops doing what is right. And they do what is evil. Then they will die because of it. But suppose a sinful person turns away from the evil things they have done. And they do what is fair and right. Then they will live by doing that.

Ezekiel 33:14-19 NIRV

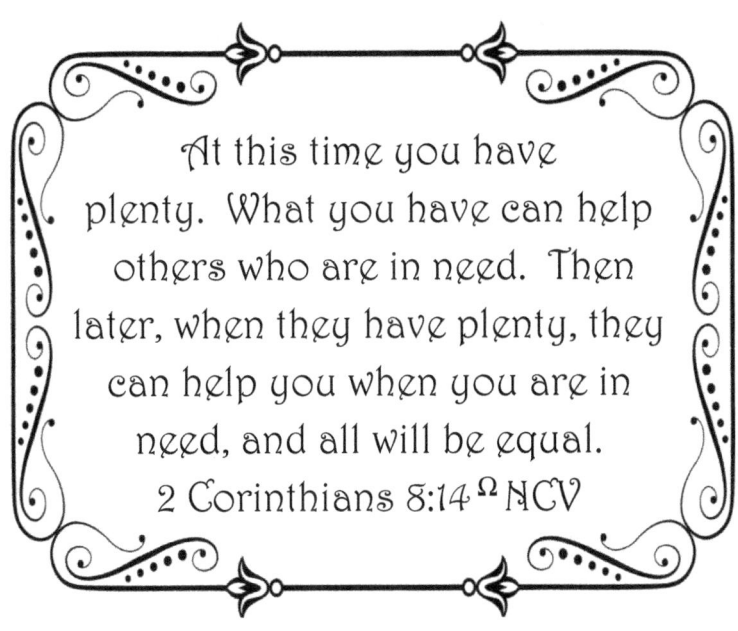

At this time you have plenty. What you have can help others who are in need. Then later, when they have plenty, they can help you when you are in need, and all will be equal.
2 Corinthians 8:14 NCV

God has shown us how kind he is by coming to save all people. Titus 2:11 CEV

You are loved.

You are treasured.

Trust

Faith's most severe tests come not when we see nothing, but when we see a stunning array of evidence that seems to prove our faith vain. –Elisabeth Elliot

GOD'S LOVE FOR LGBTQI

*They won't be afraid of bad news;
their hearts are steady because
they trust the Lord.*
Psalm 112:7 NCV

And those who know your name put their trust in you, for you, O Lord, have not forsaken those who seek you. Psalm 9:10 ESV

The Lord is my strength and my shield; my heart trusts in Him, and I am helped. Therefore my heart rejoices, and I praise Him with my song. Psalm 28:7 HCSB

For the word of the Lord is right, and all His work is trustworthy. Psalm 33:4 HCSB

Trust in the Lord with all your heart, and do not rely on your own understanding; think about Him in all your ways, and He will guide you on the right paths.
Proverbs 3:5-6 HCSB

GOD'S LOVE FOR LGBTQI

The Lord said to Moses, "How long will these people despise Me? How long will they not trust in Me despite all the signs I have performed among them?
Numbers 14:11∞ HCSB

They received help against these enemies because they cried out to God in battle, and the Hagrites and all their allies were handed over to them. He granted their request because they trusted in Him.
1 Chronicles 5:20∞ HCSB

I say to the Lord, "You are my place of safety, my fortress. My God, I trust in you." Psalm 91:2° ERV

I love your word. Time and again it has been proven true. Psalm 119:140∞ ERV

When you are angry, do not sin. Think about these things quietly as you go to bed. Selah. Do what is right as a sacrifice to the Lord and trust the Lord.
Psalm 4:4-5∞ NCV

But I have trusted in Your faithful love; my heart will rejoice in Your deliverance. Psalm 13:5∞ HCSB

Our fathers trusted in You; they trusted, and You rescued them. They cried to You and were set free; they trusted in You and were not disgraced. Psalm 22:4-5* HCSB

You will keep the mind that is dependent on You in perfect peace, for it is trusting in You. Isaiah 26:3* HCSB

But I trust in You, Lord; I say, "You are my God." Psalm 31:14* HCSB

For our hearts rejoice in Him because we trust in His holy name. Psalm 33:21* HCSB

I waited patiently for the Lord, and He turned to me and heard my cry for help. He brought me up from a desolate pit, out of the muddy clay, and set my feet on a rock, making my steps secure. He put a new song in my mouth, a hymn of praise to our God. Many will see and fear and put their trust in the Lord. How happy is the man who has put his trust in the Lord and has not turned to the proud or to those who run after lies! Lord my God, You have done many things—Your wonderful works and Your plans for us; none can compare with You. If I were to report and speak of them, they are more than can be told. Psalm 40:1-5* HCSB

The instructions of the Lord are perfect, reviving the soul. The decrees of the Lord are trustworthy, making wise the simple. Psalm 19:7∞ NLT

Do not be agitated by evildoers; do not envy those who do wrong. For they wither quickly like grass and wilt like tender green plants. Trust in the Lord and do what is good; dwell in the land and live securely. Take delight in the Lord, and He will give you your heart's desires. Commit your way to the Lord; trust in Him, and He will act, making your righteousness shine like the dawn, your justice like the noonday. Be silent before the Lord and wait expectantly for Him; do not be agitated by one who prospers in his way, by the man who carries out evil plans. Refrain from anger and give up your rage; do not be agitated—it can only bring harm. For evildoers will be destroyed, but those who put their hope in the Lord will inherit the land. A little while, and the wicked person will be no more; though you look for him, he will not be there. But the humble will inherit the land and will enjoy abundant prosperity.
Psalm 37:1-11∞ HCSB

I hate those who are devoted to worthless idols, but I trust in the Lord. Psalm 31:6∞ HCSB

Trust in Him at all times, you people; pour out your hearts before Him. God is our refuge. Selah. Psalm 62:8∞ HCSB

Faithful are the wounds of a friend; but the kisses of an enemy are deceitful. Proverbs 27:6∞ KJV

When I am afraid, I will trust in You. In God, whose word I praise, in God I trust; I will not fear. What can man do to me? Psalm 56:3-4∞ HCSB

Happy is the person who trusts in You, Lord of Hosts! Psalm 84:12∞ HCSB

Many heartaches await wicked people, but mercy surrounds those who trust the Lord. Psalm 32:10∞ GW

It is better to trust the Lord for protection than to trust anyone else, including strong leaders. Psalm 118:8-9∞ CEV

The laws you have made are fair. They can be completely trusted. Psalm 119:138∞ NIRV

Everything the Lord does is glorious and majestic, and his power to bring justice will never end. The Lord God is famous for his wonderful deeds, and he is kind and merciful. He gives food to his worshipers and always keeps his agreement with them. He has shown his mighty power to his people and has given them the lands of other nations. God is always honest and fair, and his laws can be trusted. They are true and right and will stand forever. God rescued his people, and he will never break his agreement with them. He is fearsome and holy.
Psalm 111:3-9∞ CEV

Those who trust in the Lord are like Mount Zion. It cannot be shaken; it remains forever.
Psalm 125:1∞ HCSB

Don't trust in your power to take things by force. Don't think you will gain anything by stealing. And if you become wealthy, don't put your trust in riches.
Psalm 62:10∞ ERV

I will praise the Lord all my life; I will sing praises to my God as long as I live. Do not put your trust in princes or other people, who cannot save you. When people die, they are buried. Then all of their plans come to an end. Happy are those who are helped by the God of Jacob. Their hope is in the Lord their God. He made heaven and earth, the sea and everything in it. He remains loyal forever. He does what is fair for those who have been wronged. He gives food to the hungry. The Lord sets the prisoners free. The Lord gives sight to the blind. The Lord lifts up people who are in trouble. The Lord loves those who do right. Psalm 146:2-8∞ NCV

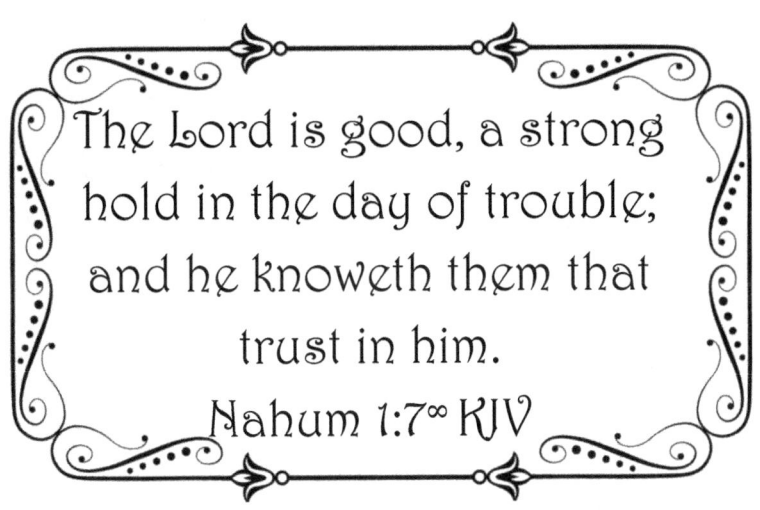

The Lord is good, a strong hold in the day of trouble; and he knoweth them that trust in him.
Nahum 1:7 KJV

Those who listen to instruction will prosper; those who trust the Lord will be joyful.
Proverbs 16:20 NLT

You can trust God.

You were made for a purpose.

Sorrow

Worrying is carrying tomorrow's load with today's strength- carrying two days at once. It is moving into tomorrow ahead of time. Worrying doesn't empty tomorrow of its sorrow, it empties today of its strength. –Corrie ten Boom

*I am sad and hurting, God,
lift me up and save me!*
Psalm 69:29 ERV

Insults have broken my heart,
and I am in despair. I waited for sympathy,
but there was none; for comforters,
but found no one. Psalm 69:20 HCSB

Be gracious to me, Lord, because I
am in distress; my eyes are worn out
from angry sorrow— my whole being
as well. Psalm 31:9 HCSB

Let your broken heart show your sorrow;
tearing your clothes is not enough."
Come back to the Lord your God.
He is kind and full of mercy;
he is patient and keeps his promise;
he is always ready to forgive
and not punish. Joel 2:13 GNT

Why did I have to be born? Was it just to suffer
and die in shame? Jeremiah 20:18 CEV

There is a time for everything,
and everything on earth
has its special season.
There is a time to be born and a time to die.
There is a time to plant and a time
to pull up plants.
There is a time to kill and a time to heal.
There is a time to destroy and a time to build.
There is a time to cry and a time to laugh.
There is a time to be sad and a time to dance.
There is a time to throw away stones
and a time to gather them.
There is a time to hug and a time not to hug.
There is a time to look for something
and a time to stop looking for it.
There is a time to keep things
and a time to throw things away.
There is a time to tear apart
and a time to sew together.
There is a time to be silent and a time to speak.
There is a time to love and a time to hate.
There is a time for war and a time for peace.
Ecclesiastes 3:1-14 ∞ NCV

My eyes are almost blind from my grief.
My whole body is as thin as a shadow.
Job 17:7∞ ERV

Death, like ocean waves, surrounded me,
and I was almost swallowed by its flooding waters.
Ropes from the world of the dead had coiled around
me, and death had set a trap in my path.
I was in terrible trouble when I called out to you,
but from your temple you heard me
and answered my prayer.
2 Samuel 22:5-7∞ CEV

I rise before dawn and cry out for help; I put my hope in Your word. Psalm 119:147∞ HCSB

For the sadness that is used by God brings a change of heart that leads to salvation—and there is no regret in that! But sadness that is merely human causes death.
2 Corinthians 7:10 Ω GNT

O Lord, how long will you forget me? Forever? How long will you look the other way? How long must I struggle with anguish in my soul, with sorrow in my heart every day? How long will my enemy have the upper hand? Turn and answer me, O Lord my God! Restore the sparkle to my eyes, or I will die. Don't let my enemies gloat, saying, "We have defeated him!" Don't let them rejoice at my downfall. But I trust in your unfailing love. I will rejoice because you have rescued me. I will sing to the Lord because he is good to me. Psalm 13:1-6∞ NLT

How long shall I take counsel in my soul, having sorrow in my heart daily? How long shall mine enemy be exalted over me? Psalm 13:2∞ KJV

Laughter cannot mask a heavy heart. When the laughter ends, the grief remains.
Proverbs 14:13∞ TLB

You saved me from death. You saved my eyes from tears and my feet from stumbling. Psalm 116:8∞ GW

My tears have been my food day and night, while they say to me all the day long, "Where is your God?"
Psalm 42:3 ESV

My anguish, my anguish! I writhe in agony! Oh, the pain in my heart! My heart pounds; I cannot be silent. For you, my soul, have heard the sound of the ram's horn— the shout of battle.
Jeremiah 4:19 HCSB

Many are the sorrows of the wicked, but steadfast love surrounds the one who trusts in the Lord. Psalm 32:10 ESV

"Lord, hear my prayer. Listen to my cry for help. Pay attention to my weeping. I'm like an outsider in your home. I'm just a stranger, like all my family who lived before me.
Psalm 39:12 NIRV

They repay me evil for good, To the sorrow of my soul. Psalm 35:12° AMP

I am weary from my groaning; with my tears I dampen my pillow and drench my bed every night. My eyes are swollen from grief; they grow old because of all my enemies. Depart from me, all evildoers, for the Lord has heard the sound of my weeping. The Lord has heard my plea for help; the Lord accepts my prayer. All my enemies will be ashamed and shake with terror; they will turn back and suddenly be disgraced. Psalm 6:6-10∞ HCSB

For I am ready to fall, And my sorrow is continually before me. Psalm 38:17∞ NASB

Why are you cast down, O my soul, and why are you in turmoil within me? Hope in God; for I shall again praise him, my salvation Psalm 42:5∞ ESV

I will say to God, my rock, "Why have You forgotten me? Why must I go about in sorrow because of the enemy's oppression?" My adversaries taunt me, as if crushing my bones, while all day long they say to me, "Where is your God?" Why am I so depressed? Why this turmoil within me? Put your hope in God, for I will still praise Him, my Savior and my God. Psalm 42:9-11∞ HCSB

Even if you look, you won't see anyone who cares enough to walk beside me. There is no place to hide, and no one who really cares. Psalm 142:4∞ CEV

Our lives last seventy years or, if we are strong, eighty years. Even the best of them are struggle and sorrow; indeed, they pass quickly and we fly away. Psalm 90:10∞ HCSB

I would have despaired had I not believed that I would see the goodness of the Lord In the land of the living. Psalm 27:13∞ AMP

You keep track of all my sorrows. You have collected all my tears in your bottle. You have recorded each one in your book. Psalm 56:8∞ NLT

And David said to Gad, "I am in great distress. Please let us fall into the hand of the Lord, for His mercies are great; but do not let me fall into the hand of man." 2 Samuel 24:14∞ NKJV

Those who plant in tears will harvest with shouts of joy. Psalm 126:5∞ NLT

O God, you are my God; earnestly I seek you; my soul thirsts for you; my flesh faints for you, as in a dry and weary land where there is no water. Psalm 63:1∞ ESV

Be gracious to me, Lord, for I am weak; heal me, Lord, for my bones are shaking; my whole being is shaken with terror. And You, Lord—how long? Turn, Lord! Rescue me; save me because of Your faithful love. Psalm 6:2-4∞ HCSB

Therefore they shall come and sing in the height of Zion, Streaming to the goodness of the Lord— For wheat and new wine and oil, For the young of the flock and the herd; Their souls shall be like a well-watered garden, And they shall sorrow no more at all.
Jeremiah 31:12∞ NKJV

He will swallow up death forever! The Sovereign Lord will wipe away all tears. He will remove forever all insults and mockery against his land and people. The Lord has spoken! Isaiah 25:8∞ NLT

Your sun will no longer set,
and your moon will not fade; for the Lord will be
your everlasting light, and the days of your sorrow
will be over.
Isaiah 60:20∞ HCSB

You are not alone.

Jesus hears your pain.

GOD'S LOVE FOR LGBTQI

Love

Love is a commitment that will be tested in the most vulnerable areas of spirituality, a commitment that will force you to make some very difficult choices. It is a commitment that demands that you deal with your lust, your greed, your pride, your power, your desire to control, your temper, your patience, and every area of temptation that the Bible clearly talks about. It demands the quality of commitment that Jesus demonstrates in His relationship to us. –Ravi Zacharias

I am absolutely sure that not even death or life can separate us from God's love. Not even angels or demons, the present or the future, or any powers can separate us. Not even the highest places or the lowest, or anything else in all creation can separate us. Nothing at all can ever separate us from God's love. That's because of what Christ Jesus our Lord has done. Romans 8:38-39 NIRV

There is no fear in love; but perfect love casts out fear, because fear involves torment. But he who fears has not been made perfect in love. 1 John 4:18 NKJV

Answer me, Lord, out of the goodness of your love; in your great mercy turn to me. Psalm 69:16 NIV

𝒟o not owe anyone anything, except to love one another, for the one who loves another has fulfilled the law. Romans 13:8 ᵒ HCSB

For God hath not given us the spirit of fear; but of power, and of love, and of a sound mind. 2 Timothy 1:7 ᵒ KJV

For we are His creation, created in Christ Jesus for good works, which God prepared ahead of time so that we should walk in them. Ephesians 2:10 ᵒ HCSB

We have thought of Your lovingkindness, O God, in the midst of Your temple. Psalm 48:9 ᵒ MEV

He saved us because of his mercy, and not because of any good things that we have done. God washed us by the power of the Holy Spirit. He gave us new birth and a fresh beginning. Titus 3:5 ᵒ CEV

Better is a dish of vegetables where love is than a fattened ox served with hatred. Proverbs 15:17 ∞ NASB

𝐵ut whoever loves God is known by God. 1 Corinthians 8:3 ᵒ NIRV

Your love must be real. Hate what is evil. Hold on to what is good. Romans 12:9 ᵒ ICB

Jesus said to them, "If God were your Father, you would love me, for I came from God and I am here. I came not of my own accord, but he sent me. John 8:42 Ω ESV

Love the Lord your God with all your heart, all your soul, all your mind, and all your strength.' The second command is this: 'Love your neighbor as you love yourself.' There are no commands more important than these."
Mark 12:30-31 Ω NCV

For when we place our faith in Christ Jesus, there is no benefit in being circumcised or being uncircumcised. What is important is faith expressing itself in love.
Galatians 5:6 Ω NLT

He should remember that the Lord does not reject people forever. When he punishes, he also has mercy. He has mercy because of his great love and kindness.
Lamentations 3:31-32 ∞ ERV

GOD'S LOVE FOR LGBTQI

I may speak in different languages, whether human or even of angels. But if I don't have love, I am only a noisy bell or a ringing cymbal. I may have the gift of prophecy, I may understand all secrets and know everything there is to know, and I may have faith so great that I can move mountains. But even with all this, if I don't have love, I am nothing. I may give away everything I have to help others, and I may even give my body as an offering to be burned. But I gain nothing by doing all this if I don't have love. Love is patient and kind. Love is not jealous, it does not brag, and it is not proud. Love is not rude, it is not selfish, and it cannot be made angry easily. Love does not remember wrongs done against it. Love is never happy when others do wrong, but it is always happy with the truth. Love never gives up on people. It never stops trusting, never loses hope, and never quits. Love will never end. But all those gifts will come to an end—even the gift of prophecy, the gift of speaking in different kinds of languages, and the gift of knowledge. These will all end because this knowledge and these prophecies we have are not complete. But when perfection comes, the things that are not complete will end. When I was a child, I talked like a child, I thought like a child, and I made plans like a child. When I became a man, I stopped those childish ways. It is the same with us. Now we see God as if we are looking at a reflection in a mirror. But then, in the future, we will see him right before our eyes. Now I know only a part, but at that time I will know fully, as God has known me. So these three things continue: faith, hope, and love.
And the greatest of these is love.

1 Corinthians 13:1-13 Ω ERV

Thus says the Lord: "Let not the wise man boast in his wisdom, let not the mighty man boast in his might, let not the rich man boast in his riches, but let him who boasts boast in this, that he understands and knows me, that I am the Lord who practices steadfast love, justice, and righteousness in the earth. For in these things I delight, declares the Lord."
Jeremiah 9:23-24∞ ESV

As for you, O Lord, you will not restrain your mercy from me; your steadfast love and your faithfulness will ever preserve me! Psalm 40:11∞ ESV

May mercy, peace, and love be yours in abundance! Jude 1:2$^\Omega$ ISV

Therefore I say to you, her sins, which are many, are forgiven, for she loved much. But he who is forgiven little loves little." Luke 7:47 $^\Omega$ MEV

I look at your heavens, which you made with your fingers. I see the moon and stars, which you created. But why are people even important to you? Why do you take care of human beings? You made them a little lower than the angels and crowned them with glory and honor. Psalm 8:3-5∞ NCV

For God so loved the world, that he gave his only begotten Son, that whosoever believeth in him should not perish, but have everlasting life. John 3:16 Ω KJV

However, due to your abundant mercy you did not do away with them altogether; you did not abandon them. For you are a merciful and compassionate God. Nehemiah 9:31∞ NET

Assyria can't save us. We won't trust in our war horses. Our own hands have made statues of gods. But we will never call them our gods again. We are like children whose fathers have died. But you show us your tender love." Then the Lord will answer, "My people always wander away from me. But I will put an end to that. My anger has turned away from them. Now I will love them freely.
Hosea 14:3-4° NIRV

If you love only the people who love you, what praise should you get? Even sinners love the people who love them. Luke 6:32 Ω NCV

Therefore also now, saith the Lord, turn ye even to me with all your heart, and with fasting, and with weeping, and with mourning: and rend your heart, and not your garments, and turn unto the Lord your God: for he is gracious and merciful, slow to anger, and of great kindness, and repenteth him of the evil. Joel 2:12-13∞ KJV

For the Father Himself loves you, because you have loved Me, and have believed that I came from God. John 16:27 Ω MEV

Then the Lord God said, "It is not good that the man should be alone; I will make him a helper fit for him." Genesis 2:18∞ ESV

But God is rich in mercy, and he loved us very much. We were spiritually dead because of all we had done against him. But he gave us new life together with Christ. (You have been saved by God's grace.) Yes, it is because we are a part of Christ Jesus that God raised us from death and seated us together with him in the heavenly places. God did this so that his kindness to us who belong to Christ Jesus would clearly show for all time to come the amazing richness of his grace. I mean that you have been saved by grace because you believed. You did not save yourselves; it was a gift from God. You are not saved by the things you have done, so there is nothing to boast about. God has made us what we are. In Christ Jesus, God made us new people so that we would spend our lives doing the good things he had already planned for us to do.

Ephesians 2:1-10 ERV

And we know that all things work together for good to them that love God, to them who are the called according to his purpose. Romans 8:28 KJV

But I tell you to love your enemies and pray for anyone who mistreats you. Matthew 5:44 CEV

You are worthy of love.

You were created to be loved by God.

Forgiveness

Perhaps it is our fear of getting our hopes up; it seems too good to be true. Perhaps it's been the almost total focus on sin and the Cross. But the Scripture is abundant and clear: Christ came not only to pardon us, but also to heal us. He wants the glory restored. So, put the book down for just a moment, and let this sink in: Jesus can, and wants to, heal your heart.
—John Eldredge

GOD'S LOVE FOR LGBTQI

O Lord, you are so good, so ready to forgive, so full of unfailing love for all who ask for your help.
Psalm 86:5° NLT

Be merciful to me, O God, because of your constant love. Because of your great mercy wipe away my sins! Psalm 51:1∞ GNT

For I will forgive their wickedness and will remember their sins no more.
Hebrews 8:12 Ω GNT

Who is a God like you? You forgive sin and overlook the rebellion of your faithful people. You will not be angry forever, because you would rather show mercy. Micah 7:18∞ GW

You forgave the evil things your people did. You took away all their sins.
Psalm 85:2∞ NIRV

Lord, show us your faithful love. Save us.
Psalm 85:7∞ NIRV

To him all the prophets bear witness that everyone who believes in him receives forgiveness of sins through his name." Acts 10:43 Ω GNT

He who believes in Him is not judged; he who does not believe has been judged already, because he has not believed in the name of the only begotten Son of God. John 3:18 Ω NASB

I correct and punish everyone I love. So make up your minds to turn away from your sins. Listen! I am standing and knocking at your door. If you hear my voice and open the door, I will come in and we will eat together. Revelation 3:19-20 Ω CEV

I have seen what they do, but I will heal them anyway! I will lead them. I will comfort those who mourn, Isaiah 57:18 ∞ NLT

All you who live anywhere on earth, turn to me and be saved. I am God. There is no other God. Isaiah 45:22 ∞ NIRV

You are ready to rescue everyone who worships you, so that you will live with us in all of your glory. Psalm 85:9 ∞ CEV

Be kind and loving to each other. Forgive each other the same as God forgave you through Christ.
Ephesians 4:32 Ω ERV

For it is by grace you have been saved, through faith—and this is not from yourselves, it is the gift of God—
Ephesians 2:8 Ω NIV

For I will forgive their wickedness and will remember their sins no more." Hebrews 8:12 Ω GNT

Seek the Lord while he may be found; call on him while he is near. Let the wicked forsake their ways and the unrighteous their thoughts. Let them turn to the Lord, and he will have mercy on them, and to our God, for he will freely pardon.
Isaiah 55:6-7 Ω NIV

The Law came, so that the full power of sin could be seen. Yet where sin was powerful, God's kindness was even more powerful. Sin ruled by means of death. But God's kindness now rules, and God has accepted us because of Jesus Christ our Lord. This means that we will have eternal life. Romans 5:20-21 Ω CEV

But if we confess our sins to God, he will keep his promise and do what is right: he will forgive us our sins and purify us from all our wrongdoing. *1 John 1:9* Ω *GNT*

Christ sacrificed his life's blood to set us free, which means that our sins are now forgiven. Christ did this because God was so kind to us. God has great wisdom and understanding, and by what Christ has done, God has shown us his own mysterious ways. Then when the time is right, God will do all that he has planned, and Christ will bring together everything in heaven and on earth. Ephesians 1:7-10 Ω CEV

"Blessed are those whose lawless deeds are forgiven, and whose sins are covered; Romans 4:7 ESV

Here is a true statement that should be accepted without question: Christ Jesus came into the world to save sinners, and I am the worst of them.
1 Timothy 1:15 ERV

God gives forgiveness.

He turns our mess into our message.

Joy

Jesus promised his disciples three things—that they would be completely fearless, absurdly happy, and in constant trouble. -G.K. Chesterton

How happy I am because of your promises— as happy as someone who finds rich treasure.
Psalm 119:162 GNT

His anger lasts only a moment, but his kindness lasts for a lifetime. Crying may last for a night, but joy comes in the morning. Psalm 30:5 NCV

These people won't give much thought to their brief lives because God keeps them occupied with the joy in their hearts.
Ecclesiastes 5:20 GW

You make known to me the path of life; in your presence there is fullness of joy; at your right hand are pleasures forevermore. Psalm 16:11 ESV

But let all those that put their trust in thee rejoice: let them ever shout for joy, because thou defendest them: let them also that love thy name be joyful in thee.
Psalm 5:11 KJV

Sometimes God gives a person wealth and possessions. God makes it possible for that person to enjoy them. God helps them accept the life he has given them. God helps them to be happy in their work. All these things are gifts from God. A person like that doesn't have to think about how their life is going. That's because God fills their heart with joy. Ecclesiastes 5:19-20∞ NIRV

Then my head will be high above my enemies around me; I will offer sacrifices in His tent with shouts of joy. I will sing and make music to the Lord.
Psalm 27:6∞ HCSB

Let those who worship him rejoice in his glory. Let them sing for joy even in bed!
Psalm 149:5° ICB

Be glad in the Lord and rejoice, O righteous, and shout for joy, all you upright in heart. Psalm 32:11∞ NRSV

And my soul shall be joyful in the Lord: it shall rejoice in his salvation.
Psalm 35:9° KJV

Light is sweet, and it is pleasing for the eyes to see the sun. Ecclesiastes 11:7∞ HCSB

Go, eat your bread with joy, and drink your wine with a merry heart, for God has already approved what you do.
Ecclesiastes 9:7∞ ESV

Give me back the joy that comes from being saved by you. Give me a spirit that obeys you so that I will keep going. Psalm 51:12∞ NIRV

My soul, praise the Lord and never forget how kind he is! Psalm 103:2∞ GW

Make a joyful noise to the Lord, all the earth; break forth into joyous song and sing praises! Sing praises to the Lord with the lyre, with the lyre and the sound of melody! With trumpets and the sound of the horn make a joyful noise before the King, the Lord! Let the sea roar, and all that fills it; the world and those who dwell in it! Let the rivers clap their hands; let the hills sing for joy together Psalm 98:4-8∞ ESV

Deceit is in the heart of those who devise evil, but those who plan peace have joy. Proverbs 12:20 ESV

Come and listen, all you who fear God, and I will tell you what he did for me. For I cried out to him for help, praising him as I spoke. If I had not confessed the sin in my heart, the Lord would not have listened. But God did listen! He paid attention to my prayer.
Psalm 66:16-19 NLT

Make a joyful shout to God, all the earth! Sing out the honor of His name; Make His praise glorious. Say to God, "How awesome are Your works! Through the greatness of Your power Your enemies shall submit themselves to You.
Psalm 66:1-3 NKJV

Be happy and sing to God, our strength. Shout with joy to the God of Jacob. Begin the music. Play the tambourines. Play the pleasant harps and lyres. Blow the ram's horn at the time of the new moon and at the time of the full moon, when our festival begins. Psalm 81:1-3 ERV

Praise be to the God and Father of our Lord Jesus Christ. God is the Father who is full of mercy. And he is the God of all comfort. 2 Corinthians 1:3 ICB

Make a joyful noise to the Lord, all the earth! Serve the Lord with gladness! Come into his presence with singing! Know that the Lord, he is God! It is he who made us, and we are his; we are his people, and the sheep of his pasture. Enter his gates with thanksgiving, and his courts with praise! Give thanks to him; bless his name! For the Lord is good; his steadfast love endures forever, and his faithfulness to all generations. Psalm 100:1-5 ESV

I will sing forever about the Lord's love. I will sing about his faithfulness forever and ever! I will say, "Your faithful love will last forever. Your loyalty is like the sky—there is no end to it!" Psalm 89:1-2 ERV

The people who walked in darkness have seen a great light; those who lived in a land of deep darkness— on them light has shined. You have multiplied the nation, you have increased its joy; they rejoice before you as with joy at the harvest, as people exult when dividing plunder. For the yoke of their burden, and the bar across their shoulders, the rod of their oppressor, you have broken as on the day of Midian. Isaiah 9:2-4 NRSV

When the Lord restored the fortunes of Zion,
we were like those who dream. Then our mouth was filled
with laughter, and our tongue with shouts of joy; then they
said among the nations, "The Lord has done great things
for them." The Lord has done great things for us; we are
glad. Restore our fortunes, O Lord, like streams in the
Negeb! Those who sow in tears shall reap with shouts of
joy! He who goes out weeping, bearing the seed for
sowing, shall come home with shouts of joy, bringing his
sheaves with him. Psalm 126:1-6∞ ESV

Your arm has great power. Your hand is strong.
Your right hand is lifted up. Your kingdom is built on
what is right and fair. Love and truth are in all you
do. Happy are the people who know how to praise
you. Lord, let them live in the light of your presence.
In your name they rejoice all the time. They praise
your goodness. Psalm 89:13-16∞ ICB

Come, let's sing for joy to the Lord.
Let's shout praises to the Rock who saves us. Let's
come to him with thanksgiving. Let's sing songs to him.
The Lord is the great God. He is the great King over all
gods. The deepest places on earth are his. And the
highest mountains belong to him. The sea is his
because he made it. He created the land with
his own hands. Psalm 95:1-5∞ ICB

Oh sing to the Lord a new song, for he has done
marvelous things! His right hand and his holy arm
have worked salvation for him. Psalm 98:1∞ ESV

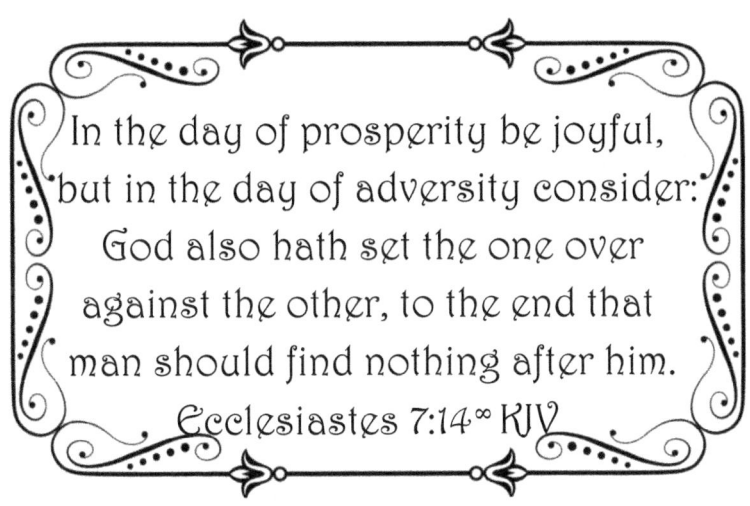

In the day of prosperity be joyful, but in the day of adversity consider: God also hath set the one over against the other, to the end that man should find nothing after him.
Ecclesiastes 7:14 KJV

But the joy that you have given me is more than they will ever have with all their grain and wine.
Psalm 4:7 GNT

You were designed to know joy.

Happiness pales in comparison to joy.

Hope

God does not waste an ounce of our pain or a drop of our tears; suffering doesn't come our way for no reason, and He seems efficient at using what we endure to mold character. If we are malleable, He takes our bumps and bruises and shapes them into something beautiful. -Frank E. Peretti

So my heart is happy, and the words I speak are words of joy. Yes, even my body will live with hope. Acts 2:26 Ω ERV

Call to me and I will answer you, and will tell you great and hidden things that you have not known. Jeremiah 33:3 ∞ ESV

Be strong and courageous, all you who put your hope in the Lord.

Psalm 31:24 ∞ HCSB

Guide me in your truth and teach me, for you are God my Savior, and my hope is in you all day long.
Psalm 25:5 ∞ NIV

God is not like people. He tells no lies. He is not like humans. He doesn't change his mind. When he says something, he does it. When he makes a promise, he keeps it.
Numbers 23:19 ∞ GW

I wait for the Lord, my soul doth wait, and in his word do I hope. Psalm 130:5 ∞ KJV

If they obey and serve him, they shall spend their days in prosperity, and their years in pleasures.
Job 36:11 ∞ KJV

I ask that your minds may be opened to see his light, so that you will know what is the hope to which he has called you, how rich are the wonderful blessings he promises his people, and how very great is his power at work in us who believe. This power working in us is the same as the mighty strength which he used when he raised Christ from death and seated him at his right side in the heavenly world.
Ephesians 1:18-20 Ω GNT

He paid attention to me. So I will call to him for help as long as I live. Psalm 116:2 ∞ NCV

I put my hope in You, Lord;
You will answer, Lord my God.
Psalm 38:15 ~ HCSB

No one who hopes in you will ever be put to shame, but shame will come on those who are treacherous without cause. Psalm 25:3 ~ NIV

Be strong and courageous, all you who put your hope in the Lord. Psalm 31:24 ~ HCSB

So the poor have hope, and injustice shuts her mouth.
Job 5:16 ~ ESV

God sent his Son into the world not to judge the world, but to save the world through him.
John 3:17 Ω NLT

Be joyful in hope, patient in trouble, and persistent in prayer. Romans 12:12 Ω ISV

GOD'S LOVE FOR LGBTQI

Lord God, you are my hope. I have trusted you since I was young. Psalm 71:5∞ ICB

Yet if you devote your heart to him and stretch out your hands to him, if you put away the sin that is in your hand and allow no evil to dwell in your tent, then, free of fault, you will lift up your face; you will stand firm and without fear. You will surely forget your trouble, recalling it only as waters gone by. Life will be brighter than noonday, and darkness will become like morning. You will be secure, because there is hope; you will look about you and take your rest in safety.
Job 11:13-18∞ NIV

Let him bury his face in the dust; perhaps there is hope. Lamentations 3:29∞ NET

Sustain me as You promised, and I will live; do not let me be ashamed of my hope. Psalm 119:116° HCSB

Therefore, since we have been justified through faith, we have peace with God through our Lord Jesus Christ, through whom we have gained access by faith into this grace in which we now stand. And we boast in the hope of the glory of God. Not only so, but we also glory in our sufferings, because we know that suffering produces perseverance; perseverance, character; and character, hope. And hope does not put us to shame, because God's love has been poured out into our hearts through the Holy Spirit, who has been given to us. Romans 5:1-5 Ω NIV

Surely there is a future, and your hope will not be cut off. Proverbs 23:18° ESV

Blessed are the merciful, for they shall receive mercy. Matthew 5:7 Ω NASB

What shall we say about such wonderful things as these? If God is for us, who can ever be against us? Romans 8:31 Ω NLT

Brothers and sisters, we don't want you to be ignorant about those who have died. We don't want you to grieve like other people who have no hope.
1 Thessalonians 4:13 ᴼ GW

He rescues the poor from the cutting words of the strong, and rescues them from the clutches of the powerful. And so at last the poor have hope, and the snapping jaws of the wicked are shut.
Job 5:15-16 ∞ NLT

For I know the plans I have for you," declares the Lord, "plans to prosper you and not to harm you, plans to give you hope and a future.
Jeremiah 29:11 ∞ NIV

Now faith is the substance of things hoped for, the evidence of things not seen. Hebrews 11:1 ᴼ KJV

Truly the eye of the Lord is on those who fear him, on those who hope in his steadfast love, Psalm 33:18 ∞ NRSV

Now, Lord, what do I wait for? My hope is in You.
Psalm 39:7 ∞ HCSB

He gives strength to the weary
and increases the power of the weak.
Even youths grow tired and weary,
and young men stumble and fall;
but those who hope in the Lord
will renew their strength.
They will soar on wings like eagles;
they will run and not grow weary,
they will walk and not be faint.
Isaiah 40:29-31∞ NIV

but the Lord takes pleasure in those who fear him, in those who hope in his steadfast love.
Psalm 147:11∞ NRSV

The thought of my suffering and homelessness is bitter beyond words. I will never forget this awful time, as I grieve over my loss. Yet I still dare to hope when I remember this: The faithful love of the Lord never ends! His mercies never cease. Great is his faithfulness; his mercies begin afresh each morning. I say to myself, "The Lord is my inheritance; therefore, I will hope in him!" The Lord is good to those who depend on him, to those who search for him.

Lamentations 3:19-25 NLT

For God alone my soul waits in silence,
for my hope is from him.
Psalm 62:5∞ NRSV

For God chose to save us through our Lord Jesus Christ, not to pour out his anger on us. Christ died for us so that, whether we are dead or alive when he returns, we can live with him forever. 1 Thessalonians 5:9-10 Ω NLT

I will give you a new heart and put a new spirit in you; I will remove from you your heart of stone and give you a heart of flesh. Ezekiel 36:26∞ NIV

Now in this hope we were saved, yet hope that is seen is not hope, because who hopes for what he sees? But if we hope for what we do not see, we eagerly wait for it with patience. Romans 8:24-25 Ω HCSB

If you declare with your mouth, "Jesus is Lord," and believe in your heart that God raised him from the dead, you will be saved. Romans 10:9 Ω NIV

Do not waste time arguing over godless ideas and old wives' tales. Instead, train yourself to be godly. "Physical training is good, but training for godliness is much better, promising benefits in this life and in the life to come." This is a trustworthy saying, and everyone should accept it. This is why we work hard and continue to struggle, for our hope is in the living God, who is the Savior of all people and particularly of all believers.

1 Timothy 4:7-10 Ω NLT

But from there you will seek the Lord your God, and you will find Him if you search for Him with all your heart and all your soul. Deuteronomy 4:29 ∞ AMP

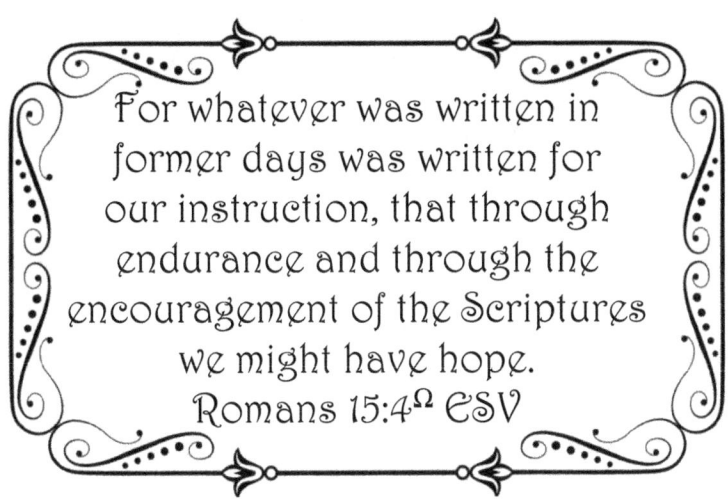

For whatever was written in former days was written for our instruction, that through endurance and through the encouragement of the Scriptures we might have hope.
Romans 15:4 ESV

We must hold on to the hope we have, never hesitating to tell people about it. We can trust God to do what he promised. Hebrews 10:23 ERV

You were meant to hope.

You are valuable.

GOD'S LOVE FOR LGBTQI

Eternity

If we find ourselves with a desire that nothing in this world can satisfy, the most probable explanation is that we were made for another world. -C.S. Lewis

I am creating a new heaven and a new earth. The troubles of the past will be forgotten. No one will remember them. Isaiah 65:17 ERV

When people sin, they earn what sin pays—death. But God gives his people a free gift—eternal life in Christ Jesus our Lord. Romans 6:23 ERV

He has made everything beautiful in its time. He has also set eternity in the human heart; yet no one can fathom what God has done from beginning to end.
Ecclesiastes 3:11 NIV

Have you not known? Have you not heard? The Lord is the everlasting God, the Creator of the ends of the earth. He does not faint or grow weary; his understanding is unsearchable. Isaiah 40:28 ESV

In the past God spoke to our ancestors many
times and in many ways through the prophets, but in
these last days he has spoken to us through his Son. He is
the one through whom God created the universe, the one
whom God has chosen to possess all things at the end.
Hebrews 1:1-2 ῼ GNT

What we see now is like a dim image in a mirror; then we
shall see face-to-face. What I know now is only partial;
then it will be complete—as complete as God's knowledge
of me. 1 Corinthians 13:12 ῼ GNT

These are only a few of the amazing things God has
done. We hear only a small whisper of God's
thundering power." Job 26:14 ∞ ERV

Then I saw a new heaven and a new earth.
The first heaven and the first earth had disappeared.
Now there was no sea. And I saw the holy city, the
new Jerusalem, coming down out of heaven from
God. It was prepared like a bride dressed for her
husband. I heard a loud voice from the throne. It
said, "Now God's home is with people. He will live
with them. They will be his people. God himself will
be with them and will be their God. He will wipe
away every tear from their eyes. There will be no
more death, sadness, crying, or pain. All the old ways
are gone." The one who was sitting on the throne
said, "Look, I am making everything new!" Then he
said, "Write this, because these words are true and
can be trusted." Revelation 21:1-5 ῼ ERV

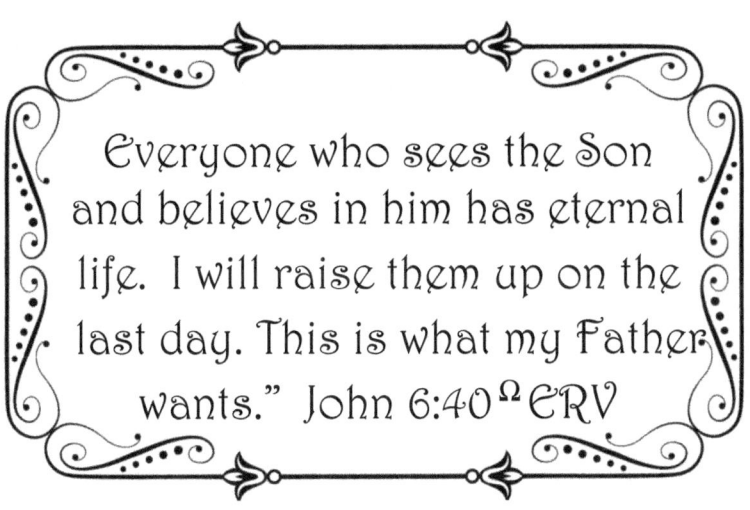

"Everyone who sees the Son and believes in him has eternal life. I will raise them up on the last day. This is what my Father wants." John 6:40 Ω ERV

But you rule forever, Lord. Your kingly chair lasts forever and ever. Lamentations 5:19 ∞ ERV

Life is only boot camp.

Living begins in eternity.

GOD'S LOVE FOR LGBTQI

Jesus Said

"Ask, and it will be given to you; seek, and you will find; knock, and it will be opened to you. For everyone who asks receives, and the one who seeks finds, and to the one who knocks it will be opened. Or which one of you, if his son asks him for bread, will give him a stone? Or if he asks for a fish, will give him a serpent? If you then, who are evil, know how to give good gifts to your children, how much more will your Father who is in heaven give good things to those who ask him! "So whatever you wish that others would do to you, do also to them, for this is the Law and the Prophets. Matthew 7:7-12 ᵒ ESV

In a loud voice Jesus said: Everyone who has faith in me also has faith in the one who sent me. And everyone who has seen me has seen the one who sent me. I am the light that has come into the world. No one who has faith in me will stay in the dark. I am not the one who will judge those who refuse to obey my teachings. I came to save the people of this world, not to be their judge. But everyone who rejects me and my teachings will be judged on the last day by what I have said. I don't speak on my own. I say only what the Father who sent me has told me to say. I know that his commands will bring eternal life. That is why I tell you exactly what the Father has told me.
John 12:44-50 $^\Omega$ CEV

Seeing the crowds, he went up on the mountain, and when he sat down, his disciples came to him. And he opened his mouth and taught them, saying:

"Blessed are the poor in spirit, for theirs
is the kingdom of heaven.
"Blessed are those who mourn,
for they shall be comforted.
"Blessed are the meek,
for they shall inherit the earth.
"Blessed are those who hunger and thirst for
righteousness, for they shall be satisfied.
"Blessed are the merciful,
for they shall receive mercy.
"Blessed are the pure in heart,
for they shall see God.
"Blessed are the peacemakers,
for they shall be called sons of God.
"Blessed are those who are persecuted for
righteousness' sake,
for theirs is the kingdom of heaven.
"Blessed are you when others revile you
and persecute you and utter all kinds of
evil against you falsely on my account.

Rejoice and be glad, for your reward is great in heaven, for so they persecuted the prophets who were before you.

Matthew 5:1-12 Ω ESV

Everyone whom the Father gives me will come to me. I will never turn away anyone who comes to me. John 6:37 Ω GW

"Do not think I have come to get rid of what is written in the Law or in the Prophets. I have not come to do this. Instead, I have come to fulfill what is written. Matthew 5:17 Ω NIRV

"You have heard that it was said, 'Love your neighbor and hate your enemy.' But I tell you, love your enemies and pray for those who persecute you, that you may be children of your Father in heaven. He causes his sun to rise on the evil and the good, and sends rain on the righteous and the unrighteous. If you love those who love you, what reward will you get? Are not even the tax collectors doing that? And if you greet only your own people, what are you doing more than others? Do not even pagans do that? Be perfect, therefore, as your heavenly Father is perfect.
Matthew 5:43-48 Ω NIV

Place my yoke over your shoulders, and learn from me, because I am gentle and humble. Then you will find rest for yourselves because my yoke is easy and my burden is light." Matthew 11:29-30 Ω GW

> "So I tell you, don't worry about the food or drink you need to live, or about the clothes you need for your body. Life is more than food, and the body is more than clothes. Look at the birds in the air. They don't plant or harvest or store food in barns, but your heavenly Father feeds them. And you know that you are worth much more than the birds. You cannot add any time to your life by worrying about it. "And why do you worry about clothes? Look at how the lilies in the field grow. They don't work or make clothes for themselves. But I tell you that even Solomon with his riches was not dressed as beautifully as one of these flowers. God clothes the grass in the field, which is alive today but tomorrow is thrown into the fire. So you can be even more sure that God will clothe you. Don't have so little faith!
> Matthew 6:25-30 ῼ NCV

Then he got into a boat and started across the lake with his disciples. Suddenly a terrible storm came up, with waves higher than the boat. But Jesus was asleep. The disciples went to him and wakened him, shouting, "Lord, save us! We're sinking!" But Jesus answered, "O you men of little faith! Why are you so frightened?" Then he stood up and rebuked the wind and waves, and the storm subsided and all was calm. The disciples just sat there, awed! "Who is this," they asked themselves, "that even the winds and the sea obey him?" Matthew 8:23-27 ῼ TLB

As Jesus was going on down the road, he saw a tax collector, Matthew, sitting at a tax collection booth. "Come and be my disciple," Jesus said to him, and Matthew jumped up and went along with him. Later, as Jesus and his disciples were eating dinner at Matthew's house, there were many notorious swindlers there as guests! The Pharisees were indignant. "Why does your teacher associate with men like that?" "Because people who are well don't need a doctor! It's the sick people who do!" was Jesus' reply. Then he added, "Now go away and learn the meaning of this verse of Scripture, 'It isn't your sacrifices and your gifts I want—I want you to be merciful.' For I have come to urge sinners, not the self-righteous, back to God."
Matthew 9:9-13 $^\Omega$ TLB

From that time Jesus began to preach his message: "Turn away from your sins, because the Kingdom of heaven is near!" Matthew 4:17 $^\Omega$ GNT

Jesus went on to say to all of them, "If anyone wants to follow me, he must say 'no' to the things he wants. Every day he must be willing even to die on a cross, and he must follow me. Luke 9:23 $^\Omega$ ICB

141

"What is all this arguing about?" Jesus asked. One of the men in the crowd spoke up and said, "Teacher, I brought my son so you could heal him. He is possessed by an evil spirit that won't let him talk. And whenever this spirit seizes him, it throws him violently to the ground. Then he foams at the mouth and grinds his teeth and becomes rigid. So I asked your disciples to cast out the evil spirit, but they couldn't do it." Jesus said to them, "You faithless people! How long must I be with you? How long must I put up with you? Bring the boy to me." So they brought the boy. But when the evil spirit saw Jesus, it threw the child into a violent convulsion, and he fell to the ground, writhing and foaming at the mouth. "How long has this been happening?" Jesus asked the boy's father. He replied, "Since he was a little boy. The spirit often throws him into the fire or into water, trying to kill him. Have mercy on us and help us, if you can." "What do you mean, 'If I can'?" Jesus asked. "Anything is possible if a person believes." The father instantly cried out, "I do believe, but help me overcome my unbelief!" When Jesus saw that the crowd of onlookers was growing, he rebuked the evil spirit. "Listen, you spirit that makes this boy unable to hear and speak," he said. "I command you to come out of this child and never enter him again!" Then the spirit screamed and threw the boy into another violent convulsion and left him. The boy appeared to be dead. A murmur ran through the crowd as people said, "He's dead." But Jesus took him by the hand and helped him to his feet, and he stood up.

Mark 9:16-27 Ω NLT

And Jesus went throughout all the cities and villages, teaching in their synagogues and proclaiming the gospel of the kingdom and healing every disease and every affliction. When he saw the crowds, he had compassion for them, because they were harassed and helpless, like sheep without a shepherd. Then he said to his disciples, "The harvest is plentiful, but the laborers are few; therefore pray earnestly to the Lord of the harvest to send out laborers into his harvest."
Matthew 9:35-38 ESV

Seek first God's kingdom and what God wants. Then all your other needs will be met as well. So don't worry about tomorrow, because tomorrow will have its own worries. Each day has enough trouble of its own. Matthew 6:33-34 NCV

The Helper is the Spirit of truth. The people of the world cannot accept him, because they don't see him or know him. But you know him. He lives with you, and he will be in you. "I will not leave you all alone like orphans. I will come back to you. In a very short time the people in the world will not see me anymore. But you will see me. You will live because I live. John 14:17-19 ERV

"Beware of practicing your righteousness before men to be noticed by them; otherwise you have no reward with your Father who is in heaven. "So when you give to the poor, do not sound a trumpet before you, as the hypocrites do in the synagogues and in the streets, so that they may be honored by men. Truly I say to you, they have their reward in full. But when you give to the poor, do not let your left hand know what your right hand is doing, so that your giving will be in secret; and your Father who sees what is done in secret will reward you. "When you pray, you are not to be like the hypocrites; for they love to stand and pray in the synagogues and on the street corners so that they may be seen by men. Truly I say to you, they have their reward in full. But you, when you pray, go into your inner room, close your door and pray to your Father who is in secret, and your Father who sees what is done in secret will reward you. "And when you are praying, do not use meaningless repetition as the Gentiles do, for they suppose that they will be heard for their many words. So do not be like them; for your Father knows what you need before you ask Him. "Pray, then, in this way: 'Our Father who is in heaven, hallowed be Your name. 'Your kingdom come. Your will be done, on earth as it is in heaven. 'Give us this day our daily bread. 'And forgive us our debts, as we also have forgiven our debtors. 'And do not lead us into temptation, but deliver us from evil. [For Yours is the kingdom and the power and the glory forever. Amen.'] For if you forgive others for their transgressions, your heavenly Father will also forgive you. But if you do not forgive others, then your Father will not forgive your transgressions. Matthew 6:1-15 ῼ NASB

Many tax collectors and sinners came to listen to Jesus. Then the Pharisees and the teachers of the law began to complain, "Look, this man welcomes sinners and even eats with them!"

Then Jesus told them this story: "Suppose one of you has 100 sheep, but one of them gets lost. What will you do? You will leave the other 99 sheep there in the field and go out and look for the lost sheep. You will continue to search for it until you find it. And when you find it, you will be very happy. You will carry it home, go to your friends and neighbors and say to them, 'Be happy with me because I found my lost sheep!' In the same way, I tell you, heaven is a happy place when one sinner decides to change. There is more joy for that one sinner than for 99 good people who don't need to change.

"Suppose a woman has ten silver coins, but she loses one of them. She will take a light and clean the house. She will look carefully for the coin until she finds it. And when she finds it, she will call her friends and neighbors and say to them, 'Be happy with me because I have found the coin that I lost!' In the same way, it's a happy time for the angels of God when one sinner decides to change."

Then Jesus said, "There was a man who had two sons. The younger son said to his father, 'Give me now the part of your property that I am supposed to receive someday.' So the father divided his wealth between his two sons.

"A few days later the younger son gathered up all

that he had and left. He traveled far away to another country, and there he wasted his money living like a fool. After he spent everything he had, there was a terrible famine throughout the country. He was hungry and needed money. So he went and got a job with one of the people who lived there. The man sent him into the fields to feed pigs. He was so hungry that he wanted to eat the food the pigs were eating. But no one gave him anything.

"The son realized that he had been very foolish. He thought, 'All my father's hired workers have plenty of food. But here I am, almost dead because I have nothing to eat. I will leave and go to my father. I will say to him: Father, I have sinned against God and have done wrong to you. I am no longer worthy to be called your son. But let me be like one of your hired workers.' So he left and went to his father.

"While the son was still a long way off, his father saw him coming and felt sorry for him. So he ran to him and hugged and kissed him. The son said, 'Father, I have sinned against God and have done wrong to you. I am no longer worthy to be called your son.' "But the father said to his servants, 'Hurry! Bring the best clothes and put them on him. Also, put a ring on his finger and good sandals on his feet. And bring our best calf and kill it so that we can celebrate with plenty to eat. My son was dead, but now he is alive again! He was lost, but now he is found!' So they began to have a party. Luke 15:1-24 ᴼ ERV

Now when Jesus came into the district of Caesarea Philippi, he asked his disciples, "Who do people say that the Son of Man is?" And they said, "Some say John the Baptist, others say Elijah, and others Jeremiah or one of the prophets." He said to them, "But who do you say that I am?" Simon Peter replied, "You are the Christ, the Son of the living God." And Jesus answered him, "Blessed are you, Simon Bar-Jonah! For flesh and blood has not revealed this to you, but my Father who is in heaven. Matthew 16:13-17 $^\Omega$ ESV

From that time on, Jesus began to show His disciples that He must go to Jerusalem and suffer many things from the elders and chief priests and scribes, and be killed, and be raised on the third day. Then Peter took Him and began rebuking Him, saying, "Far be it from You, Lord! This shall not happen to You." But He turned and said to Peter, "Get behind Me, Satan! You are an offense to Me, for you are not mindful of the things that are of God, but those that are of men." Then Jesus said to His disciples, "If anyone will come after Me, let him deny himself, and take up his cross, and follow Me. For whoever would save his life will lose it, and whoever loses his life for My sake will find it. For what will it profit a man if he gains the whole world and loses his own soul? Or what shall a man give in exchange for his soul? For the Son of Man shall come with His angels in the glory of His Father, and then He will repay every man according to his works.
Matthew 16:21-27 $^\Omega$ MEV

Immediately he made the disciples get into the boat and go before him to the other side, while he dismissed the crowds. And after he had dismissed the crowds, he went up on the mountain by himself to pray. When evening came, he was there alone, but the boat by this time was a long way from the land, beaten by the waves, for the wind was against them. And in the fourth watch of the night he came to them, walking on the sea. But when the disciples saw him walking on the sea, they were terrified, and said, "It is a ghost!" and they cried out in fear. But immediately Jesus spoke to them, saying, "Take heart; it is I. Do not be afraid." And Peter answered him, "Lord, if it is you, command me to come to you on the water. He said, "Come." So Peter got out of the boat and walked on the water and came to Jesus. But when he saw the wind, he was afraid, and beginning to sink he cried out, "Lord, save me." Jesus immediately reached out his hand and took hold of him, saying to him, "O you of little faith, why did you doubt?" And when they got into the boat, the wind ceased. And those in the boat worshiped him, saying, "Truly you are the Son of God." And when they had crossed over, they came to land at Gennesaret. And when the men of that place recognized him, they sent around to all that region and brought to him all who were sick and implored him that they might only touch the fringe of his garment. And as many as touched it were made well. Matthew 14:22-36 Ω ESV

"See that you don't look down on one of these little ones, because I tell you that in heaven their angels continually view the face of My Father in heaven. [For the Son of Man has come to save the lost.] What do you think? If a man has 100 sheep, and one of them goes astray, won't he leave the 99 on the hillside and go and search for the stray? And if he finds it, I assure you: He rejoices over that sheep more than over the 99 that did not go astray. In the same way, it is not the will of your Father in heaven that one of these little ones perish. Matthew 18:10-14 Ω HCSB

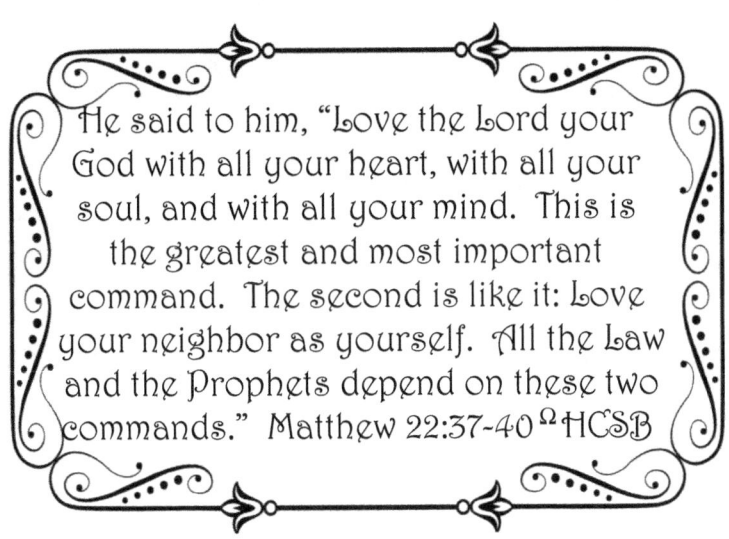

He said to him, "Love the Lord your God with all your heart, with all your soul, and with all your mind. This is the greatest and most important command. The second is like it: Love your neighbor as yourself. All the Law and the Prophets depend on these two commands." Matthew 22:37-40 ᴴCSB

If you remain in Me and My words remain in you, ask whatever you want and it will be done for you.
John 15:7 ᴴCSB

Jesus never gives up.

He is reaching out to you.

God

Do you not know? Have you not heard? The Everlasting God, the Lord, the Creator of the ends of the earth does not become tired or grow weary; there is no searching of His understanding.
Isaiah 40:28∞ AMP

You will search for me, and when you search for me with all your heart, you will find me.
Jeremiah 29:13 ERV

I, yes I, am the Lord, and there is no other Savior.
Isaiah 43:11 NLT

The Lord alone is God! He created the heavens and made a world where people can live, instead of creating an empty desert. The Lord alone is God; there are no others. The Lord did not speak in a dark secret place or command Jacob's descendants to search for him in vain. The Lord speaks the truth, and this is what he says Isaiah 45:18-19 CEV

No one has seen God at any time. The only Son, who is at the Father's side, has made Him known. John 1:18 MEV

Lord, there is no one like you. You are great! Your name is great and powerful!
Jeremiah 10:6 ERV

The grass withers and the flowers fade beneath the breath of the Lord. And so it is with people. The grass withers and the flowers fade, but the word of our God stands forever." Isiah 40:7-8∞ NLT

God's grace has saved you because of your faith in Christ. Your salvation doesn't come from anything you do. It is God's gift. Ephesians 2:8 Ω NIRV

Our Lord is great and very powerful. There is no limit to what he knows. Psalm 147:5∞ NCV

Just as the heavens are higher than the earth, my thoughts and my ways are higher than yours. "Rain and snow fall from the sky. But they don't return without watering the earth that produces seeds to plant and grain to eat. That's how it is with my words. They don't return to me without doing everything I send them to do." Isaiah 55:9-11∞ CEV

God is the one who used his power and made the earth. He used his wisdom and built the world. With his understanding he stretched the sky over the earth. God causes the loud thunder, and he causes great floods of water to fall from the sky. He makes clouds rise in the sky every place on earth. He sends lightning with the rain. He brings out the wind from his storehouses. Jeremiah 10:12-13∞ ERV

"Turn to me and be saved, all the ends of the earth! For I am God, and there is no other. Isaiah 45:22∞ ESV

"All you who live anywhere on earth, turn to me and be saved. I am God. There is no other God. Isaiah 45:22 ∞ NIRV

"For My thoughts are not your thoughts, nor are your ways My ways," declares the Lord. Isaiah 55:8 ∞ NASB

For the wages of sin is death, but the free gift of God is eternal life in Christ Jesus our Lord. Romans 6:23 Ω NASB

Since then we have a great high priest who has passed through the heavens, Jesus, the Son of God, let us hold fast our confession. For we do not have a high priest who is unable to sympathize with our weaknesses, but one who in every respect has been tempted as we are, yet without sin. Hebrews 4:14-15 Ω ESV

"And I will require the blood of anyone who takes another person's life. If a wild animal kills a person, it must die. And anyone who murders a fellow human must die. If anyone takes a human life, that person's life will also be taken by human hands. For God made human beings in his own image. Now be fruitful and multiply, and repopulate the earth."

Then God told Noah and his sons, "I hereby confirm my covenant with you and your descendants, and with all the animals that were on the boat with you—the birds, the livestock, and all the wild animals—every living creature on earth. Yes, I am confirming my covenant with you. Never again will floodwaters kill all living creatures; never again will a flood destroy the earth."

Then God said, "I am giving you a sign of my covenant with you and with all living creatures, for all generations to come. I have placed my rainbow in the clouds. It is the sign of my covenant with you and with all the earth.

When I send clouds over the earth, the rainbow will appear in the clouds, and I will remember my covenant with you and with all living creatures. Never again will the floodwaters destroy all life. When I see the rainbow in the clouds, I will remember the eternal covenant between God and every living creature on earth." Then God said to Noah, "Yes, this rainbow is the sign of the covenant I am confirming with all the creatures on earth."

The sons of Noah who came out of the boat with their father were Shem, Ham, and Japheth. (Ham is the father of Canaan.) From these three sons of Noah came all the people who now populate the earth. Genesis 9:5-19∞ NLT

As a father is kind to his children, so the Lord is kind to those who honor him. He knows what we are made of; he remembers that we are dust.
Psalm 103:13-14 ∞ GNT

But you shall hold fast to the Lord your God, as you have done to this day. For the Lord has driven out from before you great and strong nations; but as for you, no one has been able to stand against you to this day. One man of you shall chase a thousand, for the Lord your God is He who fights for you, as He promised you. Therefore take careful heed to yourselves, that you love the Lord your God.
Joshua 23:8-11 ∞ NKJV

He prayed to the Lord, "When I was still in my own country this is what I said would happen, and that is why I quickly ran away to Tarshish. I knew that you are a God who is kind and shows mercy. You don't become angry quickly, and you have great love. I knew you would choose not to cause harm.
Jonah 4:2 ∞ NCV

"God who made the world and all things in it, being Lord of heaven and earth, does not live in temples made by hands. Nor is He served by men's hands, as though He needed anything, since He gives all men life and breath and all things. He has made from one blood every nation of men to live on the entire face of the earth, having appointed fixed times and the boundaries of their habitation, that they should seek the Lord so perhaps they might reach for Him and find Him, though He is not far from each one of us. 'For in Him we live and move and have our being.' As some of your own poets have said, 'We are His offspring.'
"Therefore since we are the offspring of God, we ought not to suppose that the Deity is like gold or silver or stone or an engraved work of art or an image of the reflection of man. God overlooked the times of ignorance, but now He commands all men everywhere to repent. He has set a day when he is going to judge the world with justice, and he will use a man he has appointed to do this. God has given proof to everyone that he will do this by bringing that man back to life." Acts 17:24-31 Ω MEV

Let whoever is wise understand these things, and whoever is insightful recognize them. For the ways of the Lord are right, and the righteous walk in them, but the rebellious stumble in them. Hosea 14:9∞ HCSB

He is our God, and we are the people he cares for, his sheep that walk by his side. Listen to his voice today: *Psalm 95:7∞ ERV*

Then they will keep my laws and faithfully obey all my commands. They will be my people, and I will be their God. Ezekiel 11:20∞ GNT

The mountains quake before Him, and the hills melt; the land rises up before Him, the earth and everything that dwells on it.
Nahum 1:5∞ MEV

Oh, the depth of the riches both of the wisdom and the knowledge of God! How unsearchable His judgments and untraceable His ways! For who has known the mind of the Lord? Or who has been His counselor? *Romans 11:33-34$^\Omega$ HCSB*

"And Solomon, my son, learn to know the God of your ancestors intimately. Worship and serve him with your whole heart and a willing mind. For the Lord sees every heart and knows every plan and thought. If you seek him, you will find him. But if you forsake him, he will reject you forever. 1 Chronicles 28:9∞ NIRV

Whatever the Lord God plans to do, he tells his servants, the prophets. Amos 3:7∞ CEV

"No one can serve two masters, for either he will hate the one and love the other, or he will be devoted to the one and despise the other. You cannot serve God and money. Matthew 6:24 ∞ ESV

"And afterward, I will pour out my Spirit on all people. Your sons and daughters will prophesy, your old men will dream dreams, your young men will see visions. Even on my servants, both men and women, I will pour out my Spirit in those days. I will show wonders in the heavens and on the earth, blood and fire and billows of smoke. The sun will be turned to darkness and the moon to blood before the coming of the great and dreadful day of the Lord. And everyone who calls on the name of the Lord will be saved; on Mount Zion and in Jerusalem there will be deliverance, as the Lord has said, even among the survivors whom the Lord calls.
Joel 2:28-32∞ NIV

The Lord your God is God of all gods and Lord of all lords. He is the great God, who is strong and wonderful. He does not take sides, and he will not be talked into doing evil. Deuteronomy 10:17∞ NCV

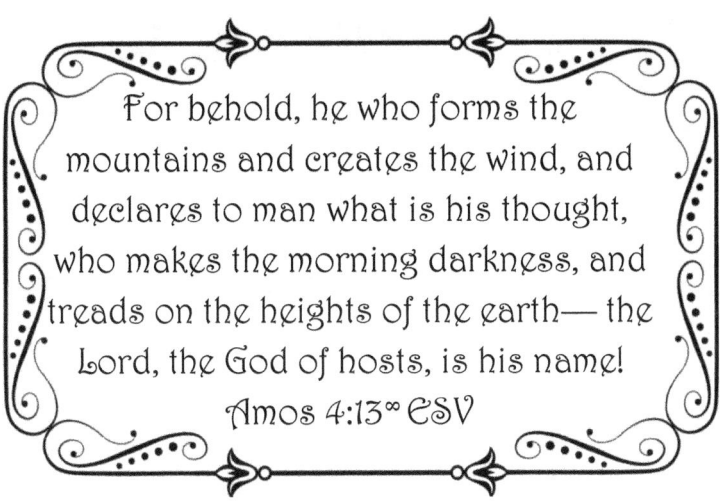
For behold, he who forms the mountains and creates the wind, and declares to man what is his thought, who makes the morning darkness, and treads on the heights of the earth— the Lord, the God of hosts, is his name! Amos 4:13ᵒ ESV

He who made the Pleiades and Orion, and turns deep darkness into the morning and darkens the day into night, who calls for the waters of the sea and pours them out on the surface of the earth, the Lord is his name; Amos 5:8ᵒ ESV

God is knowable.

You are part of something bigger.

GOD'S LOVE FOR LGBTQI

Common Questions

Nature is God's first missionary. Where there is no Bible there are sparkling stars. If a person has nothing but nature, then nature is enough to reveal something about God. –Max Lucado

GOD'S LOVE FOR LGBTQI

Does God care about people?

I look at your heavens, which you made with your fingers. I see the moon and stars, which you created. But why are people even important to you? Why do you take care of human beings? You made them a little lower than the angels and crowned them with glory and honor. Psalm 8:3-5∞ NCV

For You formed my innermost parts; You knit me [together] in my mother's womb. Psalm 139:13∞ AMP

So God created man in his own image, in the image of God created he him; male and female created he them. Genesis 1:27∞ KJV

What about people who haven't heard of Jesus?

Ever since God created the world, his invisible qualities, both his eternal power and his divine nature, have been clearly seen; they are perceived in the things that God has made. So those people have no excuse at all! Romans 1:20 Ω GNT

Is Jesus God?

The Father and I are one. John 10:30 Ω HCSB

"If you know Me, you will also know My Father. From now on you do know Him and have seen Him." John 14:7 ᵒ HCSB

In the beginning was the Word, and the Word was with God, and the Word was God. He was with God in the beginning. All things were created through Him, and apart from Him not one thing was created that has been created. Life was in Him, and that life was the light of men. That light shines in the darkness, yet the darkness did not overcome it. There was a man named John who was sent from God. He came as a witness to testify about the light, so that all might believe through him. He was not the light, but he came to testify about the light. The true light, who gives light to everyone, was coming into the world. He was in the world, and the world was created through Him, yet the world did not recognize Him. He came to His own, and His own people did not receive Him. But to all who did receive Him, He gave them the right to be children of God, to those who believe in His name, who were born, not of blood, or of the will of the flesh, or of the will of man, but of God. The Word became flesh and took up residence among us. We observed His glory, the glory as the One and Only Son from the Father, full of grace and truth. John 1:1-14 ᵒ HCSB

Jesus said to them, "I assure you: Before Abraham was, I am." John 8:58 ᵒ HCSB

Do people get into heaven by doing more good than bad?

For it is by grace you have been saved, through faith—and this is not from yourselves, it is the gift of God—not by works, so that no one can boast. Ephesians 2:8-9 Ω NIV

As it is written, There is none righteous, no, not one: Romans 3:10 Ω KJV

For the wages of sin is death, but the gift of God is eternal life in Christ Jesus our Lord. Romans 6:23 Ω HCSB

Was the Bible invented by men?

First of all, you should know this: No prophecy of Scripture comes from one's own interpretation, because no prophecy ever came by the will of man; instead, men spoke from God as they were moved by the Holy Spirit. 2 Peter 1:20-21 Ω HCSB

For the word of God is living and effective and sharper than any double-edged sword, penetrating as far as the separation of soul and spirit, joints and marrow. It is able to judge the ideas and thoughts of the heart. Hebrews 4:12 Ω HCSB

All Scripture is inspired by God and is profitable for teaching, for rebuking, for correcting, for training in righteousness, so that the man of God may be complete, equipped for every good work.
2 Timothy 3:16-17 ῼ HCSB

A Glimpse into the Bible

This is what the past is for! Every experience God gives us, every person He puts in our lives is the perfect preparation for the future that only He can see. -Corrie ten Boom

GOD'S LOVE FOR LGBTQI

If you've enjoyed the Bible verses in this book, then it might interest you to read more of the Bible. I've introduced a few chapters to get you started.

Joseph

The account of Joseph's life is one of the most amazing in the Bible. He begins his life as the son of a shepherd and ends it in the most unexpected way.

One thing that you should know before reading about Joseph is the family line that he comes from. Joseph is one of the younger sons of a man named Jacob. Jacob was a liar growing up, and after learning to trust God, his name was changed to Israel. He had twelve sons who become the twelve tribes of Israel, the ancestors of the Jewish nation.

Jacob lived in the land where his father had stayed, the land of Canaan. These are the family records of Jacob.

At 17 years of age, Joseph tended sheep with his brothers. The young man was working with the sons of Bilhah and Zilpah, his father's wives, and he brought a bad report about them to their father.

Now Israel loved Joseph more than his other sons because Joseph was a son born to him in his old age, and he made a robe of many colors for him. When his brothers saw that their father loved him more than all his brothers, they hated him and could not bring themselves to speak peaceably to him.

Then Joseph had a dream. When he told it to his brothers, they hated him even more. He said to them, "Listen to this dream I had: There we were, binding sheaves of grain in the field. Suddenly my sheaf stood up, and your sheaves gathered around it and bowed down to my sheaf."

"Are you really going to reign over us?" his brothers asked him. "Are you really going to rule us?" So they hated him even more because of his dream and what he had said.

Then he had another dream and told it to his brothers. "Look," he said, "I had another dream, and this time the sun, moon, and 11 stars were bowing down to me."

He told his father and brothers, but his father rebuked him. "What kind of dream is this that you have had?" he said. "Are your mother and brothers and I going to come and bow down to the ground before you?" His brothers were jealous of him, but his father kept the matter in mind.

His brothers had gone to pasture their father's flocks at Shechem. Israel said to Joseph, "Your brothers, you know, are pasturing the flocks at Shechem. Get ready. I'm sending you to them."

"I'm ready," Joseph replied.

Then Israel said to him, "Go and see how your brothers and the flocks are doing, and bring word back to me." So he sent him from the Valley of Hebron, and he went to Shechem.

A man found him there, wandering in the field, and asked him, "What are you looking for?"

"I'm looking for my brothers," Joseph said. "Can you tell me where they are pasturing their flocks?"

"They've moved on from here," the man said. "I heard them say, 'Let's go to Dothan.'" So Joseph set out after his brothers and found them at Dothan.

They saw him in the distance, and before he had reached them, they plotted to kill him. They said to one another, "Here comes that dreamer! Come on, let's kill him and throw him into one of the pits. We can say that a vicious animal ate him. Then we'll see what becomes of his dreams!"

When Reuben heard this, he tried to save him from them. He said, "Let's not take his life." Reuben also said to them, "Don't shed blood. Throw him into this pit in the wilderness, but don't lay a hand on him"—intending to rescue him from their hands and return him to his father.

When Joseph came to his brothers, they stripped off his robe, the robe of many colors that he had on. Then they took him and threw him into the pit. The pit was empty; there was no water in it.

Then they sat down to eat a meal. They looked up, and there was a caravan of Ishmaelites coming from Gilead. Their camels were carrying aromatic gum, balsam, and resin, going down to Egypt.

Then Judah said to his brothers, "What do we gain if we kill our brother and cover up his blood? Come, let's sell him to the Ishmaelites and not lay a hand on him, for he is our brother, our own flesh," and they agreed. When Midianite traders passed by, his brothers pulled Joseph out of the pit and sold him for 20 pieces of silver to the Ishmaelites, who took Joseph to Egypt.

When Reuben returned to the pit and saw that Joseph was not there, he tore his clothes. He went back to his brothers and said, "The boy is gone! What am I going to do?" So they took Joseph's robe, slaughtered a young goat, and dipped the robe in its blood. They sent the robe of many colors to their father and said, "We found this. Examine it. Is it your son's robe or not?"

His father recognized it. "It is my son's robe," he said. "A vicious animal has devoured him. Joseph has been torn to pieces!" Then Jacob tore his clothes, put sackcloth around his waist, and mourned for his son many days. All his sons and daughters tried to comfort him, but he refused to be comforted. "No," he said. "I will go down to Sheol to my son, mourning." And his father wept for him.

Meanwhile, the Midianites sold Joseph in Egypt to Potiphar, an officer of Pharaoh and the captain of the guard. Genesis 37:1-36∞ HCSB

Now Joseph had been taken to Egypt. An Egyptian named Potiphar, an officer of Pharaoh and the captain of the guard, bought him from the Ishmaelites who had brought him there. The Lord was with Joseph, and he became a successful man, serving in the household of his Egyptian master. When his master saw that the Lord was with him and that the Lord made everything he did successful, Joseph found favor in his master's sight and became his personal attendant. Potiphar also put him in charge of his household and placed all that he owned under his authority. From the time that he put him in charge of his household and of all that he owned, the Lord blessed the Egyptian's house because of Joseph. The Lord's blessing was on all that he owned, in his house and in his fields. He left all that he owned under Joseph's authority; he did not concern himself with anything except the food he ate.

Now Joseph was well-built and handsome. After some time his master's wife looked longingly at Joseph and said, "Sleep with me."

But he refused. "Look," he said to his master's wife, "with me here my master does not concern himself with anything in his house, and he has put all that he owns under my authority. No one in this house is greater than I am. He has withheld nothing from me except you, because you are his wife. So how could I do such a great evil and sin against God?"

Although she spoke to Joseph day after day, he refused to go to bed with her. Now one day he went into the house to do his work, and none of the household servants were there. She grabbed him by his garment and said, "Sleep with me!" But leaving his garment in her hand, he escaped and ran outside. When she saw that he had left his garment with her and had run outside, she called the household servants. "Look," she said to them, "my husband brought a Hebrew man to make fools of us. He came to me so he could sleep with me, and I screamed as loud as I could. When he heard me screaming for help, he left his garment with me and ran outside."

She put Joseph's garment beside her until his master came home. Then she told him the same story: "The Hebrew slave you brought to us came to make a fool of me, but when I screamed for help, he left his garment with me and ran outside."

When his master heard the story his wife told him—"These are the things your slave did to me"—he was furious and had him thrown into prison, where the king's prisoners were confined. So Joseph was there in prison.

But the Lord was with Joseph and extended kindness to him. He granted him favor in the eyes of the prison warden. The warden put all the prisoners who were in the prison under Joseph's authority, and he was responsible for everything that was done there. The warden did not bother with anything under Joseph's authority, because the Lord was with him, and the Lord made everything that he did successful. Genesis 39:1-23∞ HCSB

After this, the Egyptian king's cupbearer and baker offended their master, the king of Egypt. Pharaoh was angry with his two officers, the chief cupbearer and the chief baker, and put them in custody in the house of the captain of the guard in the prison where Joseph was confined. The captain of the guard assigned Joseph to them, and he became their personal attendant. And they were in custody for some time.

The Egyptian king's cupbearer and baker, who were confined in the prison, each had a dream. Both had a dream on the same night, and each dream had its own meaning. When Joseph came to them in the morning, he saw that they looked distraught. So he asked Pharaoh's officers who were in custody with him in his master's house, "Why do you look so sad today?"

"We had dreams," they said to him, "but there is no one to interpret them."

Then Joseph said to them, "Don't interpretations belong to God? Tell me your dreams."

So the chief cupbearer told his dream to Joseph: "In my dream there was a vine in front of me. On the vine were three branches. As soon as it budded, its blossoms came out and its clusters ripened into grapes. Pharaoh's cup was in my hand, and I took the grapes, squeezed them into Pharaoh's cup, and placed the cup in Pharaoh's hand."

"This is its interpretation," Joseph said to him. "The three branches are three days. In just three days Pharaoh will lift up your head and restore you to your position. You will put Pharaoh's cup in his hand the way you used to when you were his cupbearer. But when all goes well for you, remember that I was with you. Please show kindness to me by mentioning me to Pharaoh, and get me out of this prison. For I was kidnapped from the land of the Hebrews, and even here I have done nothing that they should put me in the dungeon."

When the chief baker saw that the interpretation was positive, he said to Joseph, "I also had a dream. Three baskets of white bread were on my head. In the top basket were all sorts of baked goods for Pharaoh, but the birds were eating them out of the basket on my head."

"This is its interpretation," Joseph replied. "The three baskets are three days. In just three days Pharaoh will lift up your head—from off you—and hang you on a tree. Then the birds will eat the flesh from your body."

On the third day, which was Pharaoh's birthday, he gave a feast for all his servants. He lifted up the heads of the chief cupbearer and the chief baker. Pharaoh restored the chief cupbearer to his position as cupbearer, and he placed the cup in Pharaoh's hand. But Pharaoh hanged the chief baker, just as Joseph had explained to them. Yet the chief cupbearer did not remember Joseph; he forgot him. Genesis 40:1-23∞ HCSB

Two years later Pharaoh had a dream: He was standing beside the Nile, when seven healthy-looking, well-fed cows came up from the Nile and began to graze among the reeds. After them, seven other cows, sickly and thin, came up from the Nile and stood beside those cows along the bank of the Nile. The sickly, thin cows ate the healthy, well-fed cows. Then Pharaoh woke up. He fell asleep and dreamed a second time: Seven heads of grain, plump and ripe, came up on one stalk. After them, seven heads of grain, thin and scorched by the east wind, sprouted up. The thin heads of grain swallowed up the seven plump, ripe ones. Then Pharaoh woke up, and it was only a dream.

When morning came, he was troubled, so he summoned all the magicians of Egypt and all its wise men. Pharaoh told them his dreams, but no one could interpret them for him.

Then the chief cupbearer said to Pharaoh, "Today I remember my faults. Pharaoh had been angry with his servants, and he put me and the chief baker in the custody of the captain of the guard. He and I had dreams on the same night; each dream had its own meaning. Now a young Hebrew, a slave of the captain of the guards, was with us there. We told him our dreams, he interpreted our dreams for us, and each had its own interpretation. It turned out just the way he interpreted them to us: I was restored to my position, and the other man was hanged."

Then Pharaoh sent for Joseph, and they quickly brought him from the dungeon. He shaved, changed his clothes, and went to Pharaoh.

Pharaoh said to Joseph, "I have had a dream, and no one can interpret it. But I have heard it said about you that you can hear a dream and interpret it."

"I am not able to," Joseph answered Pharaoh. "It is God who will give Pharaoh a favorable answer."

So Pharaoh said to Joseph: "In my dream I was standing on the bank of the Nile, when seven well-fed, healthy-looking cows came up from the Nile and began to graze among the reeds. After them, seven other cows—ugly, very sickly, and thin—came up. I've never seen such ugly ones as these in all the land of Egypt. Then the thin, ugly cows ate the first seven well-fed cows. When they had devoured them, you could not tell that they had devoured them; their appearance was as bad as it had been before. Then I woke up. In my dream I had also seen seven heads of grain, plump and ripe, coming up on one stalk. After them, seven heads of grain—withered, thin, and scorched by the east wind—sprouted up. The thin heads of grain swallowed the seven plump ones. I told this to the magicians, but no one can tell me what it means."

Then Joseph said to Pharaoh, "Pharaoh's dreams mean the same thing. God has revealed to Pharaoh what He is about to do. The seven good cows are seven years, and the seven ripe heads are seven years. The dreams mean the same thing. The seven thin, ugly cows that came up after them are seven years, and the seven worthless, scorched heads of grain are seven years of famine.

"It is just as I told Pharaoh: God has shown Pharaoh what He is about to do. Seven years of great abundance are coming throughout the land of Egypt. After them, seven years of famine will take place, and all the abundance in the land of Egypt will be forgotten. The famine will devastate the land. The abundance in the land will not be remembered because of the famine that follows it, for the famine will be very severe. Since the dream was given twice to Pharaoh, it means that the matter has been determined by God, and He will carry it out soon.

"So now, let Pharaoh look for a discerning and wise man and set him over the land of Egypt. Let Pharaoh do this: Let him appoint overseers over the land and take a fifth of the harvest of the land of Egypt during the seven years of abundance. Let them gather all the excess food during these good years that are coming. Under Pharaoh's authority, store the grain in the cities, so they may preserve it as food. The food will be a reserve for the land during the seven years of famine that will take place in the land of Egypt. Then the country will not be wiped out by the famine."

The proposal pleased Pharaoh and all his servants. Then Pharaoh said to his servants, "Can we find anyone like this, a man who has God's spirit in him?" So Pharaoh said to Joseph, "Since God has made all this known to you, there is no one as intelligent and wise as you are. You will be over my house, and all my people will obey your commands. Only with regard to the throne will I be greater than you." Pharaoh also said to Joseph, "See, I am placing you over all the land of Egypt." Pharaoh removed his signet ring from his hand and put it on Joseph's hand, clothed him with fine linen garments, and placed a gold chain around his neck. He had Joseph ride in his second chariot, and servants called out before him, "Abrek!" So he placed him over all the land of Egypt. Pharaoh said to Joseph, "I am Pharaoh, but no one will be able to raise his hand or foot in all the land of Egypt without your permission." Pharaoh gave Joseph the name Zaphenath-paneah and gave him a wife, Asenath daughter of Potiphera, priest at On. And Joseph went throughout the land of Egypt.

Joseph was 30 years old when he entered the service of Pharaoh king of Egypt. Joseph left Pharaoh's presence and traveled throughout the land of Egypt.

During the seven years of abundance the land produced outstanding harvests. Joseph gathered all the excess food in the land of Egypt during the seven years and put it in the cities. He put the food in every city from the fields around it. So Joseph stored up grain in such abundance—like the sand of the sea—that he stopped measuring it because it was beyond measure.

Two sons were born to Joseph before the years of famine arrived. Asenath daughter of Potiphera, priest at On, bore them to him. Joseph named the firstborn Manasseh, meaning, "God has made me forget all my hardship in my father's house." And the second son he named Ephraim, meaning, "God has made me fruitful in the land of my affliction."

Then the seven years of abundance in the land of Egypt came to an end, and the seven years of famine began, just as Joseph had said. There was famine in every country, but throughout the land of Egypt there was food. Extreme hunger came to all the land of Egypt, and the people cried out to Pharaoh for food. Pharaoh told all Egypt, "Go to Joseph and do whatever he tells you." Because the famine had spread across the whole country,

Joseph opened up all the storehouses and sold grain to the Egyptians, for the famine was severe in the land of Egypt. Every nation came to Joseph in Egypt to buy grain, for the famine was severe in every land. Genesis 41: 1-57∞ HCSB

There is so much more to this story. Eventually the same brothers who sold Joseph had to come bow before him to buy food. Only this time the brothers did not recognize Joseph because he had become a grown man and was dressed as an Egyptian.

Joseph tested his brothers and then finally...well, I'll let you read the rest of the story yourself. Just allow me to assure you that God is always at work, even when we feel like He has abandoned us. Start at Genesis 47:57 in your Bible and see what God does. My favorite verses are Genesis 50:19-20. Read until you get there.

It will be worth it.

The Ten Commandments

After God created the universe, He made the first man and woman, Adam and Eve. God made promises to them and to all people. Some of God's promises were contingent upon people's actions and others were going to happen no matter what people did. One of the things that God promised four hundred years prior to the event, was that He would rescue the descendants of Abraham from slavery in Egypt. (Genesis 15:13-16∞)

The man that God used to rescue the people from Egypt was named Moses. The book of Exodus begins with the descendants of both Abraham and his grandson Israel, becoming slaves in Egypt.

God gave them the Ten Commandments after He had delivered the people from the Egyptians. They were headed to the land that God has promised to them.

Moses summoned all of the people of Israel and said to them: Israel, listen to the laws and rules I'm telling you today. Learn them and faithfully obey them.

The Lord our God made a promise to us at Mount Horeb. He didn't make this promise to our ancestors, but to all of us who are alive here today. The Lord spoke to you face to face from the fire on the mountain. I stood between the

Lord and you to tell you the Lord's word, because you were afraid of the fire and didn't go up on the mountain. The Lord said: Deuteronomy 5:1-5∞ GW

"You shall have no other gods before me.

"You shall not make for yourself an image in the form of anything in heaven above or on the earth beneath or in the waters below. You shall not bow down to them or worship them; for I, the Lord your God, am a jealous God, punishing the children for the sin of the parents to the third and fourth generation of those who hate me, but showing love to a thousand generations of those who love me and keep my commandments.

"You shall not misuse the name of the Lord your God, for the Lord will not hold anyone guiltless who misuses his name. Deuteronomy 5:7-11∞ NIV

"Observe the day of rest as a holy day. This is what the Lord your God has commanded you. You have six days to do all your work. The seventh day is the day of rest—a holy day dedicated to the Lord your God. You, your sons, your daughters, your male and female slaves, your oxen, your donkeys—all of your animals—even the foreigners living in your city must never do any work on that day. In this way your male and female slaves can rest as you do. Deuteronomy 5:12-14∞ GW

"Honor your father and your mother, as the Lord your God has commanded you, so that you may live long and that it may go well with you in the land the Lord your God is giving you.

"You shall not murder.

"You shall not commit adultery.

"You shall not steal.

"You shall not give false testimony against your neighbor.

"You shall not covet your neighbor's wife. You shall not set your desire on your neighbor's house or land, his male or female servant, his ox or donkey, or anything that belongs to your neighbor."

These are the commandments the Lord proclaimed in a loud voice to your whole assembly there on the mountain from out of the fire, the cloud and the deep darkness; and he added nothing more. Then he wrote them on two stone tablets and gave them to me. Deuteronomy 5:16-22∞ NIV

Ruth

One of the strongest women of the Bible is a woman named Ruth. Married to a man who dies early in their marriage, she, her sister-in-law and her mother-in-law all become widows. But Ruth's strength is not only in her character, but also in her love for her mother-in-law, Naomi, and for Naomi's God.

Naomi decides to return to her former home in Bethlehem and encourages her daughters-in-law to go back to their families and remarry.

But Ruth said, "Do not urge me to leave you or turn back from following you; for where you go, I will go, and where you lodge, I will lodge. Your people shall be my people, and your God, my God. Where you die, I will die, and there I will be buried. Thus may the Lord do to me, and worse, if anything but death parts you and me." Ruth 1:16-17∞ NASB

Naomi is touched by Ruth's love for her and the two travel to Bethlehem together. Poor, widowed and disheartened, these two women cling to one another for strength and Naomi teaches Ruth the customs of the area.

Without work or money, the two survive on the scraps left over after the harvesters have picked grain. Ruth picks scraps from the field of a relative of Naomi, named Boaz.

Then Boaz said to his servant who was in charge of the reapers, "Whose young woman is this?" The servant in charge of the reapers replied, "She is the young Moabite woman who returned with Naomi from the land of Moab. And she said, 'Please let me glean and gather after the reapers among the sheaves.' Thus she came and has remained from the morning until now; she has been sitting in the house for a little while." Then Boaz said to Ruth, "Listen carefully, my daughter. Do not go to glean in another field; furthermore, do not go on from this one, but stay here with my maids. Let your eyes be on the field which they reap, and go after them. Indeed, I have commanded the servants not to touch you. When you are thirsty, go to the water jars and drink from what the servants draw."

Then she fell on her face, bowing to the ground and said to him, "Why have I found favor in your sight that you should take notice of me, since I am a foreigner?"

Boaz replied to her, "All that you have done for your mother-in-law after the death of your husband has been fully reported to me, and how you left your father and your mother and the land of your birth, and came to a people that you did not previously know. May the Lord reward your work, and your wages be full from the Lord, the God of Israel, under whose wings you have come to seek refuge." Ruth 2:5-12∞ NASB

What happens after this is a wonderful love story between two unlikely people who end up having a son named Obed, who was the father of Jesse. Jesse had a son named David, who became king over all of Israel.

Watching God's plan come to fulfillment through history in the book of Ruth will make you laugh and cry. The book of Ruth is about four pages long and well worth the read.

Job

If there is one book in the Bible that speaks to us specifically about suffering, it's the book of Job. Job is described as a man so great, that when Satan comes before the throne in heaven, God uses Job as an example. God uses Job as an example to show Satan that people who truly trust God will continue to trust Him, even when it looks like God has abandoned them.

It seems cruel to have one man suffer so much devastation—just to prove a point. But, if we look at it from a long-term perspective, perhaps other people were spared this much pain because through Job, God had already illustrated to Satan that real faith could not be shaken. Similarly we see one man suffering in the place of many, the way Jesus did—one man suffering and dying to save all people.

Job's story begins with a peek into heaven.

One day the sons of God came to present themselves before the Lord, and Satan also came with them. The Lord asked Satan, "Where have you come from?"

"From roaming through the earth," Satan answered Him, "and walking around on it."

Then the Lord said to Satan, "Have you considered My servant Job? No one else on earth is like him, a man of perfect integrity, who fears

God and turns away from evil."

Satan answered the Lord, "Does Job fear God for nothing? Haven't You placed a hedge around him, his household, and everything he owns? You have blessed the work of his hands, and his possessions have increased in the land. But stretch out Your hand and strike everything he owns, and he will surely curse You to Your face."

"Very well," the Lord told Satan, "everything he owns is in your power. However, you must not lay a hand on Job himself." So Satan left the Lord's presence. Job 1:6-12∞ HCSB

In one day Job loses every possession he has and his children are all killed. As soon as Job hears this he falls to the ground, rips his clothes, and in a surprise turn, worships God.

And said, Naked came I out of my mother's womb, and naked shall I return thither: the Lord gave, and the Lord hath taken away; blessed be the name of the Lord. In all this Job sinned not, nor charged God foolishly. Job 1:21-22∞ KJV

But these acts of destruction are not enough for Satan. In the next scene we look into heaven again.

One day the sons of God came again to present themselves before the Lord, and Satan also came with them to present himself before the Lord. The

Lord asked Satan, "Where have you come from?"

"From roaming through the earth," Satan answered Him, "and walking around on it."

Then the Lord said to Satan, "Have you considered My servant Job? No one else on earth is like him, a man of perfect integrity, who fears God and turns away from evil. He still retains his integrity, even though you incited Me against him, to destroy him without just cause."

"Skin for skin!" Satan answered the Lord. "A man will give up everything he owns in exchange for his life. But stretch out Your hand and strike his flesh and bones, and he will surely curse You to Your face."

"Very well," the Lord told Satan, "he is in your power; only spare his life." So Satan left the Lord's presence and infected Job with terrible boils from the sole of his foot to the top of his head. Then Job took a piece of broken pottery to scrape himself while he sat among the ashes.

His wife said to him, "Do you still retain your integrity? Curse God and die!"

"You speak as a foolish woman speaks," he told her. "Should we accept only good from God and not adversity?" Throughout all this Job did not sin in what he said. Job 2:1-10∞ HCSB

In an effort to console Job, his three friends go to visit him. The rest of the book of Job is a comedy of errors as each of them says that he understands why Job is going through this much hardship. One friend thinks that Job has hidden sins. Another friend says that Job just needs to ask for forgiveness. The third friend also states that Job must deserve this pain in some way.

All three of Job's friends were wrong, but they say what that any of us might have said in the same circumstance. The only way that we know they are wrong is because we were able to see into heaven for a moment.

Through thirty-seven chapters we watch Job hurting, humiliated and beside himself. But Job never curses God for what he is going through, even though he does not understand it. In the thirty-eighth chapter, God finally speaks, and everyone is silenced.

After the Lord had said those things to Job, the Lord said to Eliphaz from Teman, "I'm very angry with you and your two friends because you didn't speak what is right about me as my servant Job has done. So take seven young bulls and seven rams. Go to my servant Job, and make a burnt offering for yourselves. My servant Job will pray for you. Then I will accept his prayer not to treat you as godless fools. After all, you didn't speak what is right about me as my servant Job has done." Job 42:7-8∞ GW

After Job prayed for his friends, the Lord restored Job's prosperity and gave him twice as much as he had before. Then all his brothers and sisters and everyone who had previously known him came to him. They ate with him at his house, sympathized with him, and comforted him for all the evil the Lord had brought to him. Each one gave him some money and a gold ring.

The Lord blessed the latter years of Job's life more than the earlier years. He had 14,000 sheep and goats, 6,000 camels, 2,000 oxen, and 1,000 donkeys. He also had seven sons and three daughters. Job 42:10-13∞ GW

After this, Job lived 140 years, and saw his sons and his grandsons, four generations. And Job died, an old man and full of days. Job 42:16∞ NASB

Job's life started out well, went horribly wrong and then ended even better than it began. The dialogue between Job and his friends echoes the cries of our hearts when we feel like we are going through something unfair. When God answers, He puts things into perspective. The book of Job reminds us that we can only see a part of the picture.

God sees the whole canvas.

Psalms

Many of the Bible verses in this book came from Psalms, a book of poems and songs. One of the most fascinating aspects of this particular book is that it applies to any situation in life. If you are happy, then you will find a Psalm that fits perfectly to express your mood. On a day that you are sad, there are Psalms that express grief. When you are confused, there's a Psalm for that.

Here is Psalm 103:

Let all that I am praise the Lord;
> with my whole heart, I will praise his holy name.

Let all that I am praise the Lord;
> may I never forget the good things he does for me.

He forgives all my sins
> and heals all my diseases.

He redeems me from death
> and crowns me with love and tender mercies.

He fills my life with good things.
> My youth is renewed like the eagle's!

The Lord gives righteousness
> and justice to all who are treated unfairly.

He revealed his character to Moses
  and his deeds to the people of Israel.
The Lord is compassionate and merciful,
  slow to get angry and filled with unfailing love.
He will not constantly accuse us,
  nor remain angry forever.
He does not punish us for all our sins;
  he does not deal harshly with us, as we deserve.
For his unfailing love toward those who fear him
  is as great as the height of the heavens above the earth.
He has removed our sins as far from us
  as the east is from the west.
The Lord is like a father to his children,
  tender and compassionate to those who fear him.
For he knows how weak we are;
  he remembers we are only dust.
Our days on earth are like grass;
  like wildflowers, we bloom and die.
The wind blows, and we are gone—
  as though we had never been here.

But the love of the Lord remains forever
> with those who fear him.

His salvation extends to the children's children
> of those who are faithful to his covenant,
> of those who obey his commandments!

The Lord has made the heavens his throne;
> from there he rules over everything.

Praise the Lord, you angels,
> you mighty ones who carry out his plans,
> listening for each of his commands.

Yes, praise the Lord, you armies of angels
> who serve him and do his will!

Praise the Lord, everything he has created,
> everything in all his kingdom.

Let all that I am praise the Lord.

> Psalm 103:1-22∞ NLT

Some of the Psalms even have King David shaking his fist at God and calling down curses on his enemies. God is big enough to take our anger, our hurt and our desperation. We can talk to Him about anything.

The victim is crushed,

    and he sinks down;

        the helpless fall by their might.

The wicked say to themselves,

    "God has forgotten,

he has hidden his face,

    he will never see it."

Rise up, Lord!

    Raise your hand, God.

        Don't forget the afflicted!

Why do the wicked despise God

    and say to themselves, "God will not seek justice."?

But you do see!

    You take note of trouble and grief

        in order to take the matter into your own hand.

The helpless one commits himself to you;

    you have been the orphan's helper.

Break the arm of the wicked and evil man;

    so that when you seek out his wickedness

        you will find it no more.

The Lord is king forever and ever;

nations will perish from his land.

Lord, you heard the desire of the afflicted;

you will strengthen them,

you will listen carefully,

to do justice for the orphan and the oppressed,

so that men of the earth may cause terror no more.

Psalm 10:10-18∞ ISV

The next Psalm is one that you may recognize since it is often quoted in songs and movies. Here is Psalm 23, also called *The Lord is my Shepherd*:

The Lord is my shepherd; I shall not want.

He maketh me to lie down in green pastures:

he leadeth me beside the still waters.

He restoreth my soul:

he leadeth me in the paths of righteousness for his name's sake.

Yea, though I walk through the valley of the shadow of death, I will fear no evil:

for thou art with me;

thy rod and thy staff they comfort me.

Thou preparest a table before me in the presence of

mine enemies:

thou anointest my head with oil;

my cup runneth over.

Surely goodness and mercy shall follow me all the days of my life:

and I will dwell in the house of the Lord for ever.

Psalm 23:1-6∞ KJV

Ecclesiastes

Have you ever had one of those days? Everyone has.

One of the beautiful things about the Bible is that because it is a true account of history, it tells the good and the bad about everyone in it. This book is no exception.

The book of Ecclesiastes starts out with the author, King Solomon, pacing the floor and ranting about life. You can almost see him waving his hands as he yells out an open window;

"Meaningless! Meaningless!"

    says the Teacher.

"Utterly meaningless!

    Everything is meaningless."

What do people gain from all their labors

    at which they toil under the sun?

Generations come and generations go,

    but the earth remains forever.

The sun rises and the sun sets,

    and hurries back to where it rises.

The wind blows to the south

and turns to the north;
round and round it goes,
> ever returning on its course.

All streams flow into the sea,
> yet the sea is never full.

To the place the streams come from,
> there they return again.

All things are wearisome,
> more than one can say.

The eye never has enough of seeing,
> nor the ear its fill of hearing.

What has been will be again,
> what has been done will be done again;
> there is nothing new under the sun.

Is there anything of which one can say,
> "Look! This is something new"?

It was here already, long ago;
> it was here before our time.

> Ecclesiastes 1:2-10∞ NIV

    What follows is King Solomon analyzing each type of life. He tries out a life of indulgence. He tries being busy and he tries laying around. He tries wisdom and he tries foolishness. Nothing, he finds, makes life feel worthwhile.

As melodramatic as this short book is, there is also an air of whimsy to it. Ecclesiastes 9:9∞ NIV reads, "Enjoy life with your wife, whom you love, all the days of this meaningless life that God has given you under the sun—all your meaningless days." I laugh because he sounds like a crotchety old man who would just as soon poke you in the eye as wish you well.

In Ecclesiastes we travel with Solomon through each of these opposing experiences to find out what he has learned from each of them. He goes down some twisted roads and in the end he comes up with an odd conclusion.

This book is philosophical in nature and full of truth. I hope you will read it and see for yourself.

Paul

Paul is not a book in the Bible. However, no discussion of the Bible would be complete without mentioning him. Why? Because God used him in a powerful way and he was one of the least likely converts to Christianity.

To read about Paul we would have to start in the book of Acts; this is where we learn that Paul belonged to a Jewish religious group called the Pharisees and was happy to kill Christians. He eagerly threw Christian men and women in jail, just for believing that Jesus was the son of God. He saw Christians, called "followers of the way" as a blight on his country and his religion. During this time Paul went by the name Saul.

Paul's life was fine until the day he set out to imprison Christians in the city of Damascus and instead Jesus knocked him onto his backside. Literally. Let's see what happened:

> In the meantime Saul kept up his violent threats of murder against the followers of the Lord. He went to the High Priest and asked for letters of introduction to the synagogues in Damascus, so that if he should find there any followers of the Way of the Lord, he would be able to arrest them, both men and women, and bring them back to Jerusalem. As Saul was coming near the city of

Damascus, suddenly a light from the sky flashed around him. He fell to the ground and heard a voice saying to him, "Saul, Saul! Why do you persecute me?"

"Who are you, Lord?" he asked.

"I am Jesus, whom you persecute," the voice said. "But get up and go into the city, where you will be told what you must do."

The men who were traveling with Saul had stopped, not saying a word; they heard the voice but could not see anyone. Saul got up from the ground and opened his eyes, but could not see a thing. So they took him by the hand and led him into Damascus. For three days he was not able to see, and during that time he did not eat or drink anything. Acts 9:1-9 Ω GNT

Now Saul's pretty shaken up, but equally shaken is a man named Ananias. Ananias is a Christian in Damascus who gets tapped on the shoulder by God and told to go relate a message to Paul. And just like all of us, Ananias argues with God. Does God really know who this guy, Paul, is? You can almost hear the whine in his voice and the boom in God's when He tells Ananias to get off his duff and head over to Paul's house.

The message Ananias has to deliver to Paul sends a chill down my spine. No one would want to hear those words.

Now there was a believer in Damascus named Ananias. The Lord spoke to him in a vision, calling, "Ananias!"

"Yes, Lord!" he replied.

The Lord said, "Go over to Straight Street, to the house of Judas. When you get there, ask for a man from Tarsus named Saul. He is praying to me right now. I have shown him a vision of a man named Ananias coming in and laying hands on him so he can see again."

"But Lord," exclaimed Ananias, "I've heard many people talk about the terrible things this man has done to the believers in Jerusalem! And he is authorized by the leading priests to arrest everyone who calls upon your name."

But the Lord said, "Go, for Saul is my chosen instrument to take my message to the Gentiles and to kings, as well as to the people of Israel. And I will show him how much he must suffer for my name's sake."

So Ananias went and found Saul. He laid his hands on him and said, "Brother Saul, the Lord Jesus, who appeared to you on the road, has sent me so that you might regain your sight and be filled with the Holy Spirit." Instantly something like scales fell from Saul's eyes, and he regained his sight. Then he got up and was baptized. Acts 9:10-18 ῼ NLT

God was going to show Saul/Paul just how much he would suffer for becoming a Christian. I am sure that those words didn't comfort Paul. But God ended up giving him amazing abilities to share God's word with people and do miraculous things. He was stoned and left for dead, shipwrecked, beaten repeatedly, bitten by a venomous snake, and imprisoned in cities throughout the Roman Empire.

He did end up speaking before kings, governors and magistrates. He started churches, had visions, wrote much of the New Testament and mentored the next generation of Christian leaders. Paul lived a thrilling life, fraught with peril. And in the end he was so transformed that he said;

"For I consider that the sufferings of this present time are not worthy to be compared with the glory which shall be revealed to us." Romans 8:18 ῼ MEV.

He also said, "Our light affliction, which lasts but for a moment, works for us a far more exceeding and eternal weight of glory." 2 Corinthians 4:17 ῼ MEV.

Now that is a life that's been transformed.

That's what Jesus does.

When He enters a home He doesn't just sweep the floor, He bulldozes and erects a mansion. But don't be scared. Jesus knew Paul's heart. He knew that Paul would use his natural zeal to be zealous for Jesus. It's the same with us. God created each of us to be unique and to use those unique qualities to serve Him in a special way.

Some examples of God using a person's natural abilities for His purposes include each of the New Testament authors.

John, the author of the New Testament book named after him, was soft-spoken and loving. In the book of John, his words are kind and gentle, full of love.

God used Matthew, the author of the book of Matthew, to illustrate to the Jewish people that Jesus was the fulfillment of the Old Testament prophecies through his lineage and actions.

Mark, who wrote the gospel of Mark, gives a shortened account of Jesus' life.

And Luke, a physician, gives the kind of detailed information you'd expect from a doctor- about the healings that Jesus performed. Luke went on to write the book of Acts, which is his follow-up book, written to a man named Theophilus.

The Bible is full of amazing accounts of bravery and cowardice that make any other literature pale in comparison.

GOD'S LOVE FOR LGBTQI

Ending Prayer

Now may the God of hope fill you with all joy and peace as you believe in Him so that you may overflow with hope by the power of the Holy Spirit.
Romans 15:13 HCSB

…

I hope that by reading this book you realize that you are loved. You are not just loved by another person. You are loved by the creator of the universe. He created you with a specific purpose for your life and He can't wait for you to start living it. The first step is to invite Him into your heart. Is there anything that is keeping you from asking Jesus into your life right now?

Let's pray.

God, thank you for being so loving and kind. Thank you that You never give up on us. Thank you for sending Jesus to die a brutal death so that He could pay for every wrong thing that any human has ever done. We get to enter heaven because of what Jesus did for us.

If we wrote down every wrong thing that we have ever thought or done, it would devastate us. Our sins are too much to bear. But You said that if we confess our sins, You are faithful and just to forgive us of our sins and make us clean in Your eyes. (1 John 1:9$^\Omega$)

Erase our sins and let us start fresh with You in our lives. Help us wipe every sinful memory from our minds and help us to remember that because we ask You to- You will make us clean.

You said that whoever hears Your words from the Bible, believes that Jesus is Your son and invites

Jesus to be in their lives has passed from death into life. (John 5:24Ω) We ask for that today. Erase our sins. Free us from hurt and bondage. Rescue us and let us have a relationship with You that is beyond anything that we could ever imagine. (1 Corinthians 2:9Ω)

We ask all of this in the most powerful name under heaven, the name of Jesus. Amen. (Acts 4:12Ω)

If you would like to find out more about who Jesus is, I encourage you to start reading the book of John in the New Testament section of the Bible. The New International Version (NIV) of the Bible is written in plain English and can be found in almost any store. You can also read it online at BibleGateway.com.

You can watch free movies, find resources, ask questions and print a Bible reading plan at http://LGBTQIpromises.yolasite.com/

Recommended Reading

The Purpose Driven Life by Rick Warren

The Case for Christ by Lee Strobel

NIV Study Bible by Zondervan

Left Behind by Tim Lahaye and Jerry B. Jenkins

The Jesus I Never Knew by Philp Yancey

The Hiding Place by Corrie Ten Boom

When all is said and done, the life of faith is nothing if not an unending struggle of the spirit with every available weapon against the flesh.

-Dietrich Bonhoeffer

ABOUT THE AUTHOR

Marie White is the host of the popular YouTube series, **Bible Stories for Adults,** which reaches people in every part of the world.

She is also a missionary, traveler and lover of people. She endeavors to love people by sharing God's word..

To learn more about the Bible, watch her YouTube video series, **Bible Stories for Adults**.

For a FREE BOOK or to contact the author please visit www.MarieWhiteAuthor.com.
Facebook Marie at Marie Author, Instagram @MarieWhiteAuthorOfficial, or Tweet @LGBTQIPromises.

Like what you've read?
Try **Ten Day Bible Study** by Marie White.

Available on Amazon in paperback and Kindle editions, Barnes & Noble Nook, Apple iBook, Kobo and on Smashwords.

www.ingramcontent.com/pod-product-compliance
Lightning Source LLC
Chambersburg PA
CBHW070605300426
44113CB00010B/1408